Foundations of Business and Company Law

Sabrina Bruno

Foundations of Business and Company Law

US, UK, Italy and the European Context

Springer

Sabrina Bruno
Business and Company Law
University of Calabria and Luiss G. Carli
Rome, Italy

ISBN 978-3-031-71884-7 ISBN 978-3-031-71885-4 (eBook)
https://doi.org/10.1007/978-3-031-71885-4

This Springer imprint is published by the registered company Springer Nature Switzerland AG
The registered company address is: Gewerbestrasse 11, 6330 Cham, Switzerland

to Lea

Contents

Introduction 1

Contents

This book aims at explaining the interrelationships between economic elements and legal principles with reference to business and company law. Three jurisdictions are taken into consideration: US, UK, and Italian law (the latter chosen as a prototype of continental European legal systems). In addition, since Italy is a member state of the European Union that harmonizes, through regulations and directives, company law among European member states, an introduction to European company law will be covered by the book.[1] The economic elements that lie at the ground of business and company law are actually common to the three legal systems, and consequentially, legal principles and rules are very similar despite the fact that one jurisdiction (namely, Italy) belongs to civil law and the other two to common law legal families.[2] Similarity also depends on the historical origins of the legal instruments that are covered by the book: partnership law traces back to Roman law, while company law

[1] It is worth pointing out that there is no European Union legislation with reference to proprietorships and partnerships, subjects that are regulated by each European member state.

[2] According to the traditional classification formerly theorized by David (1964), the diversity of the world's legal systems is not random, but groups of countries share common features in terms of legal history, legal thinking, and positive rules. To summarize, the civil law family (in general) is based on Roman law, with the influence of German universities tracing back to the nineteenth century, and is characterized by the codification of laws and the consequential role of academics in the interpretation of written legislation. By contrast, common law is judge-made law, based on cases where legal precedents are binding on future cases showing similar facts (so-called principle of *stare decisis*); pragmatism is relevant. However, more recently, classification into legal families has been criticized as it does not provide an accurate picture; it might "cause more harm than good"; see Siems (2014), p. 93.

S. Bruno, *Foundations of Business and Company Law*,
https://doi.org/10.1007/978-3-031-71885-4_1

traces back to English law. Roman law and English law have influenced, respectively, the law of partnerships and of companies worldwide.

I have followed the traditional format of separating the law of proprietorships, of partnerships, and of companies. Each topic is covered by, firstly, identifying the economic and legal elements that are shared by the three jurisdictions and, then, by dealing with each jurisdiction separately for individual specificities.

It will be interesting to observe that the characteristics of the legal family have a few consequences on the legal principles and rules that have been developed in the jurisdictions with reference to business and company law. This is no surprise as modern comparative lawyers have been doubtful of the validity of some generalizations on the differences between civil law and common law: legal precedents, for example, do play a significant role in European continental legal systems; codes are less all-embracing in practice than they may be in theory, with various and different special legislation being enacted continuously along with the code.[3] In addition, written pieces of legislation are very common and frequent in the USA and UK, especially in our field of business and company law, as will be shown. However, some differences still remain. As masterfully explained with reference to English law in particular, "despite this quantitative superiority of modern legislation, it remains, in many ways, true to say that case law reflects the spirit of English law far more than legislation does"; moreover, most legislation in the UK and the US "is not drafted in the form of a statement of true principles, broad generalizations" but "in the form of a set of specific rules, *ad hoc* solutions to particular problems"; "the detailed and crabbed style of legislative drafting means that it becomes almost impossible for the Courts to draw principles from legislation."[4] Therefore, we can argue that the fundamental difference between civil law and common law is that "the common law [i.e. cases] remains the true repository of principles" and "judges . . .make the law," whereas in civil law, the true repository of principles remains the legislation. Also, the style of English cases, compared with European continental cases, is different, with the latter showing "far less detail in the analysis of the facts of cases." Furthermore, a difference lies in the role of academics under English law versus civil law (in this respect, the US is similar to civil law): under English law, the role of academics is modest, and the purpose of English textbooks is not a creative exercise; academics simply read up the law (made by judges) and try to reduce it to some sort of shape or order.[5] By contrast, in civil law and US legal systems, the opinion of academics is highly regarded and their interpretation of legal provisions very important. Finally, it will be worth noting and highlighting that, with reference to company law in particular, it is not correct to equate UK and US laws as "Anglo-Saxon" jurisdictions (as too often and too simplistically, unfortunately, it has been mystified): there are indeed fundamental differences, in company law, between these

[3] Atiyah (1987), p. 2.

[4] Atiyah (1987).

[5] Atiyah (1987).

two jurisdictions despite them both belonging to the common law family, as will be shown.

Following the same pattern in the whole book (identifying the economic elements first and then covering common legal principles and core provisions in each jurisdiction), I start by dealing with the law of proprietorship (Chap. 2). I then address the law of partnerships (Chap. 3). Moreover, I deal with company law, analyzing US (Chap. 4), UK (Chap. 5), and European company law, with a special focus on Italy (Chap. 6). The style of the book is characterized by making reference to various factual examples in presenting the topics and by often using a colloquial and dialectical language in order to make the subject more interesting and understandable, in particular for students.

The book is the result of my studies and research conducted in Italy, Great Britain (Oxford University), and the United States (Harvard Law School and Stanford Law School, primarily) during the last 30 years and more; it reflects thoughts and reflections that I have made over the years. In this respect I believe the book can be of much interest for both those who approach for the first time the study of these jurisdictions and those who want to develop or update their knowledge on them. But the book is also the outcome of my over 20 years of teaching the course of "Law and Economics (Business and Company Law)" at Luiss G. Carli University of Rome (Italy) within the Bachelor Degree of Economics and Business curriculum, which is attended by both Italian and international students. The choice of these three jurisdictions certainly depends on my past studies—as a company lawyer in my academic career, I have been mainly studying these three jurisdictions and, of course, European law—and also on the need to introduce international students, having different backgrounds, to three legal systems that are fundamental in the field of business and company law: i.e., Italian (deriving from Roman law, which shaped the law of partnerships worldwide, and, with reference to companies, mainly regulated by European company law, which therefore is common also to the other member states in many respects, as will be explained), UK (where the first form of company limited by shares was born in the seventeenth century which influenced legislations worldwide and where, more recently, in the 1990s the corporate governance debate began), and US, where the biggest corporations in the world were born and have developed.

References

Atiyah PS (1987) Pragmatism and theory in English law. Stevens & Sons, London
David R (1964) Les Grands Systèmes de Droit Contemporains. Dalloz, Paris
Siems M (2014) Comparative law. Cambridge University Press, Cambridge

2 The Sole Proprietor

Contents

2.1 Sources of Business Law in the US, UK, and Italy

Any business venture may be carried out by individuals or by a group of persons. In the first case, we have sole proprietors; in the latter case, we have partnerships or companies (corporations).

We begin with the examination of the sole proprietor, that is, the individual who owns the business that is operated. This individual *owns* the business carried out in the sense that she/he is entitled to the residual interest in the cash flows generated by the business, and she/he controls the business by having the right to decide how to manage the activities of the business.

In all the three jurisdictions under examination, we can identify a sole proprietor whenever the business activity is operated as an *organization*: in the three jurisdictions, business law starts to be applied whenever an organization exists. However, business law in the US and the UK differs from that in Italy, where there are more formal rules applying to proprietorships.

S. Bruno, *Foundations of Business and Company Law*,
https://doi.org/10.1007/978-3-031-71885-4_2

Preliminarily, let us explain what is to be considered a source of law and what these sources are in the jurisdictions under examination and with reference to sole proprietorships. A source of law is any act or fact capable of creating, amending, or extinguishing legal rules, i.e., producing law.

The sources of US and UK law, with reference to sole proprietorships, are common law (i.e., judge-made law), various pieces of legislation (e.g., the United States Bankruptcy Code, 2020; the UK Insolvency Act, 1986, etc.), and customs.

As for the sources of Italian law of proprietorships, they are the Constitution and constitutional laws, the Civil Code and ordinary statutes (i.e., special legislation), regulations and customs. The list above is in hierarchical order in the sense that a subordinate source cannot in any way dictate a rule contrary to the one enacted by a higher source. By contrast, a higher-ranking rule can repeal a lower-ranking rule. Therefore, a statute may amend a previous regulation, but a regulation may not amend a previous statute. Conflicts between rules on par with one another are resolved by reference to the chronological criterion, according to which a later rule prevails over an earlier one in time (for example, a subsequent statute overrides a prior one). The hierarchical ranking of the sources of law is the instrument by which the implementation of the fundamental principles of the legal system is guaranteed, in particular the principles enshrined in the Constitution. Among these sources, the most relevant for proprietorships and business law in general are the Civil Code, originally enacted in 1942, as amended (in particular, from Articles 2082 to 2620); special legislation such as the Code of Crisis (Legislative Decree N. 14/2019, as amended in 2020 and 2022); and customs. The foregoing sources of law can be termed "formal' in that they are specifically envisaged by Article 1 of the "Provisions on the Law in General" set forth at the beginning of the Civil Code. However, it is also necessary to take account of the sources of so-called substantial law not specifically contemplated by the Civil Code. These sources are academic opinions and case law. More precisely, by "substantial" sources of law means the interpretation of the provisions of "formal" law by courts and legal authors.

2.2 The Concept of Organization Is Alike in the Three Jurisdictions

What is the meaning of an organization? If the business venture is large and complex, involves many people other than the owner (such as suppliers, lenders, employees, etc.), comprises various material and immaterial inputs (such as capital, know-how, land, plants, etc.), and generates profits, it is an organization, and the owner is a sole proprietor, to whom business law applies. In any of the jurisdictions under examination, we do not find rules with precise identification, in quantitative terms, of such factors (as how many employees, how much capital, etc.) that explain at what point an organization starts and business law applies. Therefore, just a careful examination and evaluation of all the facts and circumstances will lead to an understanding of whether an organization exists and whether business law shall apply to the owner of the venture. It is a matter of fact, as construed by the legal doctrine and case law in the three jurisdictions.

For example, let us consider the case of Ms. Mary, who owns and operates a restaurant and devotes her full time to its management, hires just one employee, and has invested just her own money in the business. Is it an organization? Is she a sole proprietor? Does business law apply? The answers are all negative in all the jurisdictions under consideration in this book.

By contrast, if Ms. Mary owns a restaurant; delegates management (or part of it) to another person; hires 20 employees; borrows 500,000 euros, dollars, or sterling from the bank; and generates lots of profits each year, we can say that an organization exists. Again, such numbers as 20 (employees) and 500,000 (euros, dollars, or sterling) are just examples (as no specific number is set by the jurisdictions) of a significant amount of employees or capital invested, factors from which it is possible to infer that the activity is meaningful.

The concept of organization, from a factual view, is therefore equivalent in *all the jurisdictions* under examination.

2.3 The Sole Proprietor Under US Law: Definition and Formalities

Under US law, the sole proprietor is qualified by legal authors as the owner of the equity or residual interest in a business.[1] The sole proprietor can operate under the name of the owner or under a fictitious name and does not have to register with the State where she/he operates. The sole proprietor must acquire local licenses and permits to operate the business, but no other rules apply. It is common knowledge that over 70% of US businesses are owned and operated by sole proprietors.

2.4 The Sole Proprietor (or Sole Trader) Under UK Law: Definition and Formalities

The sole proprietor (or sole trader, as more commonly defined in the UK) is the owner of a business. In the UK, the sole trader is required, within 3 months of starting the activity, to register online with the HM Revenue & Customs so that a tax return shall be expected every year; however, no registration fee is involved. No other consequences derive from such registration.

Even though there is no legislative requirement, sole traders keep records and accounts. The accounts shall follow accepted accounting practices to give a true and fair view of the business; however, the exact form of the accounts is not laid down by law. This means sole traders are not required by law to produce a balance sheet; as a matter of fact, large businesses do produce balance sheets.

[1] Klein et al. (2010), p. 1.

2.5 The Sole Proprietor Under Italian Law: The Commercial Entrepreneur

Quite differently from the other two jurisdictions, the fundamental notion in Italian business law is that of a commercial entrepreneur (*imprenditore commerciale*). Why is this concept so fundamental? It is because only commercial entrepreneurs are subject to a special body of rules, known as "the statute of the commercial entrepreneur," which consists of the application of rules on:

1. Judicial liquidation
2. Keeping of accounts
3. Registration in the general section of the Register of Enterprises (*Registro delle Imprese*) at the Chamber of Commerce
4. Commercial agency (*rappresentanza commerciale*), i.e., the applicability of special agency rules that derogate from the scheme envisaged by private law in general
5. Various other miscellaneous rules

Therefore, only a commercial entrepreneur can be subject to judicial liquidation, only a commercial entrepreneur is obliged to maintain the accounting records and books of account envisaged by the Civil Code, only a commercial entrepreneur must be registered in the general section of the Register of Enterprises, and only a commercial entrepreneur is subject to the special rules on agency. Accordingly, it is necessary to identify who or what can be classified as a commercial entrepreneur.

The Civil Code does not define in express terms who or what a commercial entrepreneur is, but its Article 2082 defines the notion of an entrepreneur, and its Article 2195 lists the entrepreneurs who must be enrolled with the Register of Enterprises. Therefore, it is possible to identify a commercial entrepreneur by reading Article 2082 in conjunction with Article 2195.

Article 2082 of the Civil Code provides as follows:

> An entrepreneur is one who engages professionally in an *organised* economic activity for the production or exchange of goods or services.

The provisions of Article 2195 of the Civil Code are as follows:

> Entrepreneurs who engage in any of the following activities are obliged to enrol in the Register of Enterprises: (1) an industrial activity aimed at the production of goods or rendering of services; (2) intermediation in the trading of goods; (3) transport by land, water or air; (4) banking or insurance activities; (5) other activities ancillary to those set forth above.

The list in Article 2195 of the Civil Code is not complete but merely illustrative (for example, financial activities are not expressly mentioned). Therefore, one can say that a commercial entrepreneur is whoever satisfies the requisites laid down by

Article 2082 of the Civil Code and whoever, *for example*, pursues one of the activities listed in Article 2195 of the Civil Code. However, in order to identify a commercial entrepreneur, it is necessary to refer to two more articles: Article 2083 of the Civil Code, which defines a so-called small entrepreneur, and Article 2135 of the Civil Code, which defines a so-called agricultural entrepreneur.

Article 2083 of the Civil Code states as follows:

> Farmers who personally cultivate the land, craftsmen, small merchants and those who engage professionally in an activity involving principally their own labour and that of their family members are small entrepreneurs.

Article 2135 of the Civil Code provides as follows:

> An agricultural entrepreneur is one who engages in an activity aimed at cultivation of land, silviculture, breeding of animals or related activities. By cultivation of land, silviculture, and breeding of animals, it is meant activities directed to take care and develop a biological cycle or a necessary phase of it, of vegetal or animal nature, that use or may use land, woods or fresh, marine, or brackish waters. Related activities are those, exercised by the same entrepreneur, aimed at manipulating, preserving, transforming, selling, embellishing the agricultural products as well as aimed at offering goods or services using equipment or resources normally employed in the exercise of the agricultural activity, including activities valorising the territory and the rural and forest heritage, or reception and hospitality as defined by law (i.e. farm holidays).

A commercial entrepreneur is one who, in addition to satisfying the requisites laid down by Article 2082 of the Civil Code and engaging, for example, in one of the activities listed in Article 2195 of the Civil Code, is neither a small nor an agricultural entrepreneur. In other words, the notion of agricultural entrepreneur and small entrepreneur serves to identify *by exclusion* who or what a commercial entrepreneur is. In effect, case law considers a commercial entrepreneur as one who satisfies the conditions of Article 2082 of the Civil Code and is not either an agricultural or a small entrepreneur.

Let us now consider the specific requisites of Article 2082 of the Civil Code one by one:

1. "Engages professionally": "professionally" is to be understood in the sense of the activity being exercised on a continuous, consistent, determined, and intentional basis, as opposed to as a hobby or occasionally from time to time. For example, if a person purchases a car and then sells it 1 year later for a profit, can she/he be considered an entrepreneur? Certainly not, because the person has carried out just one transaction, and accordingly, it is not something she/he does on a continuous basis.
2. "Economic activity": "economic" means that the activity must be organized with a view to making a profit, that is, with a view to incurring costs that are lower than

revenues. It may happen that in a particular period of time (e.g., economic crisis), costs exceed revenues, but what is important to consider is whether the activity has been structured in such a way that, normally, revenues exceed costs. Some authors also consider that "economic" means that the activity shall be directed to the market, not undertaken for the benefit of the same entrepreneur. In addition, "activity" literally means a series of acts. However, in some cases, even a single act can amount to engaging in a business activity if it is of such a size that its implementation necessarily implies professional skills or substantial investments. An example in this regard might be the act of building the Channel Tunnel: although a single act in a certain sense, its size dictates that it be considered a business activity. However, whether a single act has to be considered an activity depends on a case-by-case evaluation.

3. The activity must be aimed at the production or exchange of goods and/or services in the market. That is, the object of the activity is meant to offer goods and services on the market. By contrast, self-production does not satisfy this requirement.
4. "Organised ... activity": organization is the most important element in that it distinguishes a commercial entrepreneur from a small entrepreneur, an agricultural entrepreneur, or any natural person who is not an entrepreneur. By organization means the organization of the factors of production: capital, labor, plant and equipment, etc. **Example**: Let us, for a moment, consider one of the categories of a small entrepreneur: the craftsman (see Article 2083 of the Civil Code, mentioned above). A craftsman is a person who manages to make a product using her/his personal abilities. For example, a tailor is a craftsman as she/he is able to create clothes mainly using her/his own hands, skills, and creativity. If the tailor hires and pays a number of assistants, purchases machinery to make clothes, and utilizes huge sums of capital borrowed from third parties, then she/he becomes a commercial entrepreneur. Why? It is because through the labor of others, capital, and machinery, she/he assembles together a form of organization. At that point, the clothes that will be made by the employees, the machines, etc. will be more a product, an outcome of the organization rather than the manual skills of the craftsman (see Fig. 2.1).

2.5.1 Small, Agriculture Entrepreneurs and Professionals Under Italian Law

Unlike for commercial entrepreneurs, there are no legal requirements for small and agriculture entrepreneurs; they are therefore contemplated by the Civil Code in order to identify them and distinguish them from commercial entrepreneurs. Therefore, small and agriculture entrepreneurs have no duty to keep books, accounts, and balance sheets; judicial liquidation does not apply to them in the case of insolvency; no legal representatives for them are contemplated by law (only ordinary representation rules under the Civil Code (i.e., need for a power of attorney)); and registration at the Registrar Office is in a special section provided just for statistics and with no

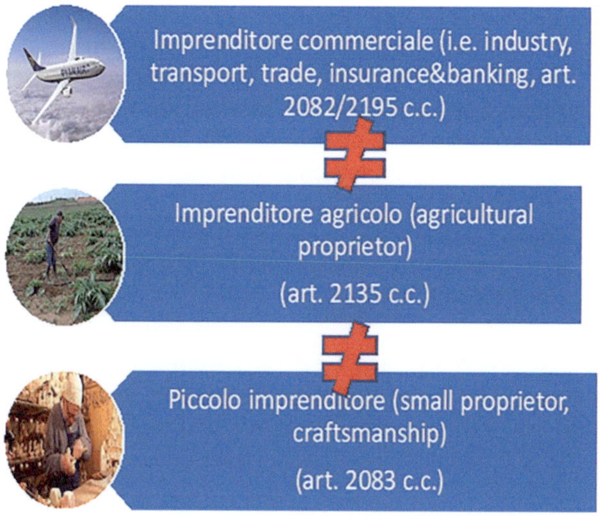

Fig. 2.1 The sole proprietor: Italian law. Source: Author's own elaboration

effect to evidence facts or acts *vis-a-vis* third parties. However, an exception for agricultural proprietors is provided because for them, despite being registered in the special section, the same special agency rules as for commercial entrepreneurs, which derogate from private law in general, apply.

Another peculiarity of Italian law refers to *professionals* (e.g., the owner of a law firm, of an accounting firm, of a health care facility, etc.) Shall professionals be qualified as commercial entrepreneurs in Italy? If we consider Article 2082 of the Civil Code, professionals seem to meet all the characteristics therein provided: they engage professionally in their activity; have an organization made of people, capital, equipment, etc.; offer services to the market; and carry out economic activity with a view to making profits. Nonetheless, they are *not* entrepreneurs under the Italian Civil Code. To them, different sections of the Civil Code apply, such as Title III on self-employment work. In particular, Articles 2222 and following on *contratto d'opera* establishing the prevalence of the professional's own work over the organization do apply, as well as Articles 2229 and following on intellectual professions providing for personal responsibility for the execution of contracts. Professionals have been ontologically conceived differently from entrepreneurs since before the Civil Code was enacted in 1942, also for cultural reasons: a sharp line was drawn by a piece of legislation dated 1936 between the two categories. Professionals have been subject to special legislation aiming at "protecting" intellectual professions by providing for certain privileges and immunities (that is why they are also defined in Italy as "protected professions")—partly abolished since. However, and this is still the case, the Civil Code, by excluding the application of the rules on commercial entrepreneurs, establishes that professionals have no duty to register, keep books and accounts, etc. and are *not* subject to judicial liquidation. In any case, Article 2238 states: "If the exercise of the profession is element of an activity organized as enterprise, Articles of Title II shall be applied." Accordingly, whenever the professional activity is part of a bigger organization of which the professional is not the owner, the owner will be deemed a commercial entrepreneur: an example is that of a doctor who works for a health care facility of a relevant size owned by another person. To the owner of the facility, the rules on commercial entrepreneurs will apply, while the doctor's activity with her/his patient will be regulated by the articles of the Civil Code on self-employment.

2.6 Sole Proprietors and Third Parties: Creditors and Judicial Liquidation

Carrying out a business activity, from a legal viewpoint, means involving other people in the business venture by entering into contracts with them (Fig. 2.2).

These third parties may become creditors to the sole proprietor. The application of judicial liquidation (also called bankruptcy) proceedings is not typical of Italian law

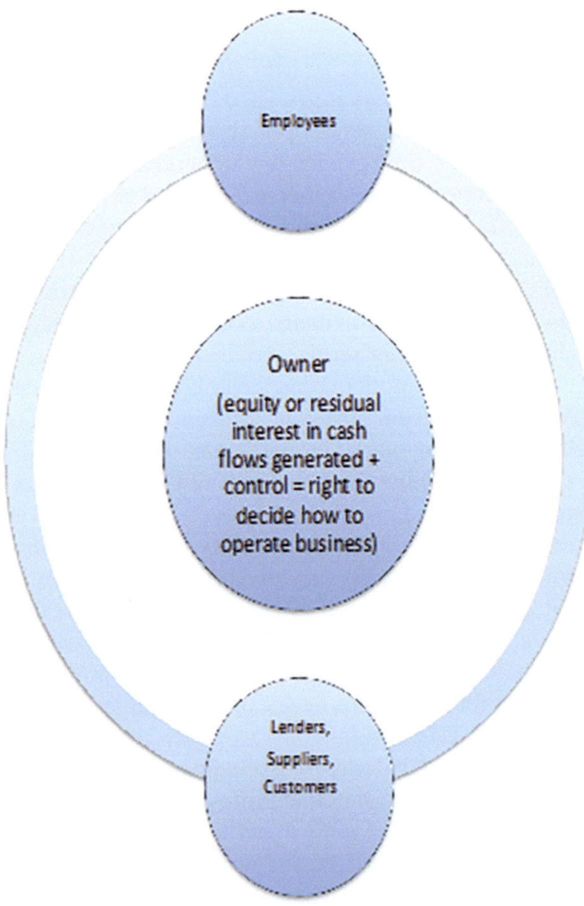

Fig. 2.2 People involved in business ventures. Source: Author's own elaboration

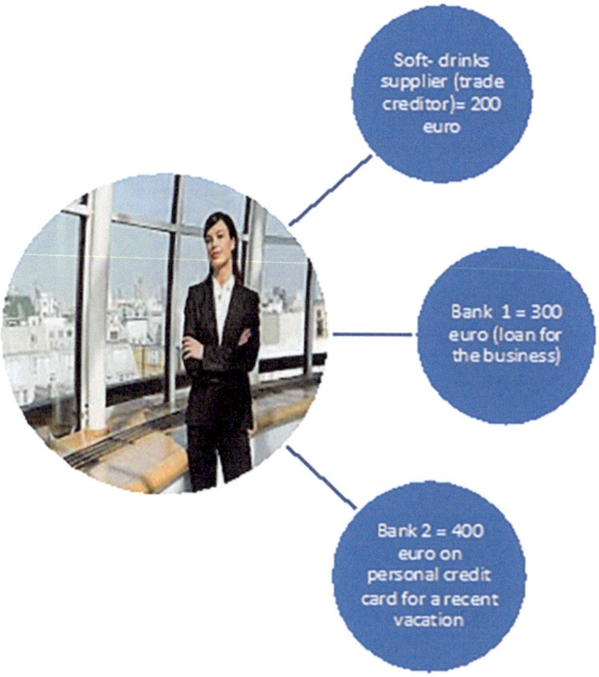

Fig. 2.3 Sole proprietors vs. creditors. Source: Author's own elaboration

but instead common to US and UK jurisdictions: the sole proprietor is personally responsible for *all* debts, lawsuits, and taxes deriving from the business, and in the case of inability to pay debts, the sole proprietor is made bankrupt. The difference between Italy, on one side, and the United States and the United Kingdom, on the other side, is that in Italy, only commercial entrepreneurs, as defined, are subject to bankruptcy, while in the United States or the United Kingdom, any debtor (even individuals, consumers, etc. and all sole proprietors, regardless of the activity exercised) can be declared bankrupt. In particular, in the United States and the United Kingdom, also professionals (lawyers, accountants, engineers, etc.) may be subject to a bankruptcy procedure, which is not the case in Italy. In other words, in the United States and the United Kingdom, "commercial activities" are in no way different from other activities, and bankruptcy may apply both to individuals and sole proprietorships whenever an organization exists.

Examples of different classes of creditors can be seen in Fig. 2.3.

As shown in Fig. 2.3, it is possible that the sole proprietor, in addition to creditors arising from the business, engages also with personal creditors (e.g., in the box above, Bank 2 for her personal credit card used for vacation). Moreover, the sole proprietor may own personal assets (e.g., the house where she/he lives, her/his personal car, etc.) and business assets (e.g., the bank account where business revenues are deposited, the building where the business activity is carried out, etc.).

However, in the event of bankruptcy, there is no distinction whatsoever between personal and business assets nor between personal and business debts (except for modest exceptions). All assets (business and personal) are in the *same pot*, and all creditors share the same pot (based on the amount owed to them). The sole distinction is between secured *versus* unsecured creditors. The former category has a privilege and shall be satisfied before unsecured creditors. This principle applies to *all jurisdictions*. According to Italian, UK, and US laws, personal liability is always associated with business: whenever a business is operated by an individual, she/he will be liable with all her/his assets (both personal and business) to satisfy business creditors.

> While under US and UK laws this is a common law principle, in Italian law, this concept is codified by Article 2740 of the Civil Code, according to which "The debtor is personally liable with *all* [his/her] *present and future* assets. Limitation of liability is allowed only in cases provided by law."

This general provision of the Italian Civil Code applies to all debtors, including sole proprietors.

Therefore, all general creditors are concerned with the business because they share the risk of default. In order to limit the risk of default, creditors need to ask for a guarantee (e.g., mortgage, pledge) from the sole proprietor to become secured creditors and be preferred over the unsecured (i.e., general) creditors. On the other hand, the sole proprietor, in the case of bankruptcy, must pay debts through her/his business assets *and* personal assets (e.g., even a villa on the beachside) until *all* creditors are satisfied.

2.6.1 US Legislation on Bankruptcy

Bankruptcy is regulated by the United States Bankruptcy Code (2020). There are different types of bankruptcies, depending on the categories of individuals or entities involved, which are usually referred to by chapters in the Code itself. The chapter of the Code dealing with the bankruptcy of sole proprietors is *Chapter 7*, which provides for liquidation, i.e., the sale of the debtor's nonexempt property and the distribution of the proceeds to creditors. The debtor may file a petition with the bankruptcy court serving the area where she/he has a principal place of business or principal assets. Together with the petition, the debtor shall file schedules of assets and liabilities, current income and expenditure, and statement of financial affairs. The Court shall appoint a bankruptcy trustee, who will gather and sell the debtor's nonexempt assets, and shall use the proceeds of such assets to pay holders of claims (i.e., creditors) in accordance with the provisions of the Bankruptcy Code and in a manner that maximizes the return to the debtor's unsecured creditors (while secured creditors will be satisfied through the original guarantee, i.e., lien, mortgage). Under this Code, by insolvency means a situation where the sum of debts is greater than all of such entity's property, at a fair valuation (Chapter 1 Section 101 para. (32) of the US Bankruptcy Code). Filing a petition automatically stops collection actions against the debtor from all creditors; this stay arises by operation of law. As long as the stay is in effect, creditors may not initiate or continue lawsuits. The trustee may also attempt to recover money or property under the trustee's "avoiding powers," which include the powers to set aside preferential transfers of property made to creditors within 90 days before the petition, to undo security interests that were not properly perfected under the law, and to pursue claims such as fraudulent conveyance and bulk transfer remedies available under state law. The Court may authorize the trustee to operate the business for a limited period of time if such operation will benefit creditors and enhance the liquidation of assets.

In order to avoid bankruptcy, debtors should consider filing a petition under Chapter 11 of the Bankruptcy Code and seek an adjustment of debts, either by reducing the debt or by extending the time for repayment, or may seek a more comprehensive reorganization. In addition, sole proprietorships may also be eligible for relief under Chapter13, which provides for an opportunity to save their homes from foreclosure by allowing them to "catch up" past due payments through a payment plan.

2.6.2 UK Legislation on Bankruptcy

In the United Kingdom, bankruptcy is regulated under the Insolvency Act 1986 (as amended), Part IX. It applies to individuals in dealing with debts they cannot pay. A bankruptcy order can be made upon the petition of the debtor or an application by creditors when the sum owed is £5000 or more. The Court shall appoint an official receiver, attached to the Court and the trustee. The trustee will take control of the debtor's assets, sell them (except for domestic items or items needed for the job), and distribute the proceeds to the creditors, who must file a formal claim. The business will be closed, and any business assets will be claimed by the trustee. Also, under UK law, secured creditors are preferred over unsecured creditors. Any money left over, after the satisfaction of the creditors, will be returned to the debtor. The trustee may attempt to recover money or property under the trustee's "avoiding powers" to set aside certain transactions identified by law.

The law provides for an individual voluntary arrangement (IVA), which is an agreement between the debtor and the creditors to pay all or part of the debts: an IVA can give the debtor more control over her/his assets than bankruptcy, and the business can be run. Usually, an insolvency practitioner will contact the creditors, and the IVA will start if the creditors holding 75% or more of the debts agree to it, and it will apply to *all* the creditors, including anyone who disagrees with it. An IVA will stop the creditors from taking action against the debtor. The IVA can be canceled by the insolvency practitioner if the debtor does not keep up with the repayments, in which case the debtor will be made bankrupt.

2.6.3 Italian Legislation on Judicial Liquidation

In Italy, insolvency procedures are regulated by the Code of Entrepreneurship Crisis and of Insolvency, in force since 2022.

Two are the conditions to be subject to judicial liquidation:

1. Being a commercial entrepreneur (as mentioned above)
2. Being insolvent

All commercial entrepreneurs are subject to judicial liquidation unless they show due debts not exceeding 30,000 euros. As for the meaning of insolvency, it occurs whenever the entrepreneur is not able to *regularly* satisfy claims. According to case law and legal authors, "regularly" means timely compliance with debts. For example, if on the balance sheet the liabilities exceed the assets, this does not mean that the entrepreneur is automatically insolvent in so far as she/he can get additional financing to regularly pay debts. On the contrary, if on the balance sheet the assets exceed the liabilities, insolvency cannot be by itself excluded because if assets are illiquid, they cannot be used to pay debts. Therefore, insolvency cannot be inferred from the balance sheet, but it is a matter of fact and consists in whether a commercial entrepreneur is insolvent or not; it really depends on her/his possibility to satisfy creditors on time.

Judicial liquidation is declared by the Court upon the request of the debtor, one or more creditors, or the public minister. The effects of the judgment, after having verified that the prerequisites mentioned above occur, are as follows:

1. All the debtor's assets, personal and business, will be in the same pot, to be shared with all creditors (*par condicio creditorum* = equal treatment among all creditors).
2. The creditors' individual claims are immediately stopped.
3. The business activity is stopped.
4. A trustee in bankruptcy (*curatore*) is appointed by the court, who will be in charge of satisfying the creditors' claims, taking into account the distinction between secured and unsecured creditors (so-called ranking of claims), through liquidation of assets. By liquidation means the sale of a debtor's property and the distribution of the proceeds to the creditors.

According to Italian law, judicial liquidation is the procedure of last resort for entrepreneurs in case alternative procedures cannot be pursued. Alternative procedures shall be started whenever the entrepreneur is insolvent but prospects of turning around the financial crisis occur. They are regulated by the Code of Crisis and include compositions with creditors, plans of turning around, restructuring agreements, and administrative receivership (*Concordato preventivo*).

2.7 Sole Proprietors and Third Parties: Employees

Another category involved in a business venture is employees. Rules between sole proprietors and employees are not part of business law but part of *labor and private laws*. Employment relationships can be regulated by union rules, contracts, or individualized written agreements in the three jurisdictions we are analyzing. Obviously, entering into individualized agreements implies incurring transaction and information costs, as for any contract.

In an employment relationship, in the three jurisdictions, it is possible to identify the master and the servant. The former has the *right to control* the latter and the power to terminate the agreement. Another possibility is to make an agency contract between the sole proprietor and the third party, in which case the former is the principal while the latter is the agent; agents owe a duty of loyalty (no self-interest) to principals, which is part of the broader *fiduciary obligations* concept (which will be analyzed in Section 3.2.3 below).

A consequence of this relationship is the so-called *vicarious liability*, which means that the employer (i.e., the sole proprietor) is liable to pay damages suffered by third parties when the unlawful act arises from the employee's conduct within the performance of her/his duties.

Example

Suppose an employee, while performing her/his duties, negligently injures a customer. From whom can the customer recover damages? With or without fault of the employee? According to the vicarious liability principle, the answer is that damages can be recovered from the employer (i.e., the sole proprietor) even in the case of fault of the employee and even in the case of lack of fault from the employer (it is a form of strict liability). Vicarious liability arises by virtue of the relationship. The reason is to protect third parties from damages caused by organizations in the assumption that employers have greater financial resources than employees and that the imposition of vicarious liability promotes the deterrence of tortious conduct by providing incentives for employers to exercise not only the right but also the *duty to control* employees. However, the availability of insurance also played a significant role in the development of vicarious liability. Vicarious liability also applies to agency contracts.

While the vicarious liability principle has been developed by case law in the United States and the United Kingdom, in Italy, the rule is stated in the Civil Code.

Article 2049 of the Civil Code provides as follows:

Masters and principals are liable for damages of their servants and agents caused by fraudulent or negligent acts within the exercise of their functions.

Reference

Klein WA, Coffee JC Jr, Partnoy F (2010) Business, organization and finance. Thomson Reuters, New York

Joint Ownerships: Partnerships

3

Contents

S. Bruno, *Foundations of Business and Company Law*,
https://doi.org/10.1007/978-3-031-71885-4_3

3.1 Meaning of Joint Ownership: Elements Common to the Three Jurisdictions

A business activity can be operated by individuals (sole proprietors) or, collectively, by two or more people, in which case we have partnerships (or companies). In this section, we will analyze what the considerations and the economic reasons are that bring potential sole proprietors to carry out a business activity collectively rather than individually and as partnerships.

If you have an interest in engaging in an economic activity, why would you need to manage firms jointly? Reasons can be to collect more capital and resources, to gain more expertise or know-how on the specific business, or to share risk.

But can't you borrow money from the bank rather than share ownership of the business with another person to collect more capital? In this case, capital would be not in the form of equity but in the form of debt. The difference is that with equity, the person would be the residual claimant: i.e., she/he would get big gains, if any, but with a higher risk of loss than with debt.

In addition, if you need a different expertise, can't you hire employees or consultants instead of sharing ownership with another person? And with reference to risk, couldn't you agree with the bank that lends you some money to share risk with you, as well as a percentage of the profits? In the latter case, you could still manage the business by yourself. But in this scenario, the bank or another third party that agrees to lend you money and share risk would require something else, i.e., control over the business. As the amount of debt increases in relation to equity, at some point, the lender would be subject to all risks of losses of the business; therefore, the lender would require control over the management. Without control, the lender may fear asymmetry of information and moral hazard by the sole proprietor. In addition, people (i.e., banks) that are willing to lend money might require the business to be financed with enough equity capital to feel secure against any risk of default: therefore, this may involve asking two or more equity investors to pool their resources, in which case there would be a partnership anyhow. Above all, entering into such agreements (with employees, consultants, the bank, etc.) would mean incurring *transaction costs*. These are the reasons why it could be more convenient for a sole proprietor to set up a partnership to carry out a business activity.

As we are going to examine, if you sum up all these elements, i.e., capital, risk, profits, and control, you obtain the provisions regulating partnerships in the three jurisdictions. Sharing all these elements with one or more persons means, at law, becoming partners. By applying rules on partnerships, there are no transaction costs: instead of bargaining all such clauses (on capital, risk, profits, control)—whereby the result of the negotiation could not be just or fair or customary by itself (depending on the strength of your position)—it could be more convenient to rely upon legal norms.

There are fundamental elements that are common to the three jurisdictions we are analyzing. Partnerships are usually characterized by being made of a *few partners*. Generally, small firms and *small businesses* are carried out through partnerships. Examples of small businesses are agriculture, craftsmanship, professional services (legal, computing, design, architecture, accounting, etc.), and trade. In addition, the relationship among partners is based upon *mutual trust and reliance* (also said with the Latin expression *affectio societatis*). In other words, how would you choose your partner in a business? Since you are going to share control, risk, and profits with the other partners, you should rely on them. Setting up a partnership means undertaking a continuous relationship with all the partners; therefore, you want to be sure that the other partners are honest, capable, economically solid, etc. The personal relationship among partners is a fundamental feature of partnerships, which constitutes one of its most important differences in relation to corporations.

Because of these elements common to the three jurisdictions, the *regulation of partnerships is very similar* among the three. Another reason for this similarity is that partnership law has been influenced historically by Roman law.

The *technique* for regulation is the same: it consists in providing for *mainly default rules* that leave partners ample leeway to make express agreements designed to alter those rules. There are a few mandatory rules. The *contents* of the regulation in the three jurisdictions focus on three main topics: *control*, *agency*, and *liability*. In addition, contents consist of regulating the relationship among partners and the relationship between partnerships/partners and third parties. Another element that is common to the three jurisdictions concerns the contribution that can be made to the partnership to become partners. *Contributions* can consist of any kind of asset, such as capital (i.e., money), credit, services (e.g., consultancy, advice, etc.), property (e.g., movable or immovable), know-how, etc.

3.2 US Partnership Law: Sources of Law

General sources of law in the United States are the Constitution, federal and state statutes, administrative regulations, and case law. Federal laws are enacted by Congress and apply uniformly to all 50 states, while state legislation is enacted by the Parliament of one state and applies within it. Partnership law is regulated by states. This means that, in theory, there would be 50 different pieces of legislation on partnerships, depending on the state where the partnership has been set up. However, the Uniform Law Commission (UCL), also called the National Conference of Commissioners on Uniform State Laws—a nonprofit American association—aims to provide US states with drafted model acts in order to bring clarity and stability to statutory laws across jurisdictions, especially for areas where uniformity is desirable and practical. With reference to partnerships, the Commission adopted in 1914 the Uniform Partnership Act (UPA 1914), a model statute drafted for partnerships, which was long ago adopted in every state but for Louisiana. In 1994, the Revised Uniform Partnership Act (RUPA) was enacted, and later on, there were various revisions to the Uniform Partnership Act (the last was in 2013), but most of the core concepts of UPA 1914 remained; there were no significant variations. However,

[1] For the text of the Uniform Partnership Act, see http://source.gosupra.com/docs/statute/224#.

RUPA was not adopted by all states. The consequential situation is that the law of partnerships is not uniform around states. Elements of commonality among states are reflected in the *Uniform Partnership Act (UPA) 1914*, and most of the existing case law arose under UPA (1914). Therefore, in presenting the regulation of partnerships, the focus of this book will be on UPA 1914.[1]

3.2.1 Definition: How to Set Up a Partnership?

According to Section 6(1) of UPA (1914),

> "A partnership is an *association* of two or more persons to carry on as co-owners a business for profit."

The association, to be set up, needs a consensual agreement, which can be express or tacit. The fundamental element is that the business is carried on as *co-owners*, that is, with the aim of sharing in the profits *and* control of it.

> **Example 1**
> A manager who works for Mary is entitled by contract to a bonus consisting of a share of profits. Is she/he a partner?

> **Example 2**
> Two people own real estate as joint tenants (i.e., a big building divided into various apartments, each apartment giving rent to the owners each month). Is this a partnership?

> **Example 3**
> A father, who is a sole proprietor of a business consisting of building various apartments in a green area and selling or renting them out, maintaining them, planting beautiful flowers, and opening various shops (for residents and nonresidents), dies. His two sons inherit the business. Does the business activity become a partnership between the two brothers?

In Example 1, the element missing to have a partnership is sharing control. The manager is entitled to a bonus, that is, just to share profits, but this is not enough to make her/him a partner. Following the definition under Section 6(1) of UPA, sharing both profits and control is required to have a partnership.

With reference to Example 2, in this case, there is no partnership either because being co-owners of a building as joint tenants does not mean carrying on a business activity. There is no exercise of *entrepreneurial activity* in the example made but just enjoyment of a common tenancy. Merely enjoying rent from the apartment each month cannot be equated to making profits: profits derive from the actual exercise of a business activity, which is not the case in the example made.

In Example 3, the situation is different because the father, as a sole proprietor, definitely exercised a business activity in the real estate sector. As for the two heirs, it depends on what they do with the real estate. If they merely enjoy the real estate and do not continue the business activity started by their father, they will be joint tenants of the real estate, enjoying rent, and there will be no partnership between them. But if they keep on investing in the real estate operating like their father used to do, a partnership is born between them. And it is important to stress that a partnership is born even though the two brothers do not sign any partnership agreement—even though they do not even realize there is a partnership between them. What counts, in business law, are the factual circumstances of each case. A court that is asked to decide whether a partnership exists or not among two or more people shall carefully analyze the facts, regardless of the parties' intention or consciousness.

Why is that? This is because partnerships can be set up by a partnership agreement *or* without formality. To set up a partnership, there are no documents, no meetings, no certificates, no fees, even no realization of it required. The agreement, if any, can be made in writing or can be tacit (a handshake, a nod of the head, or even a course of action). Even if a partnership agreement is consensual in nature (it being an "agreement"), the failure of partners to label themselves as partners or even to think of themselves as partners is irrelevant. What courts shall evaluate to ascertain whether a partnership exists or not is if all these elements occur and are proven: *share of profits*, *risk*, and *control.* If all these elements are proven and there is a business activity carried on, a partnership exists, like it or not.

The *same principle*, i.e., the evaluation of the factual occurrence of all these elements, applies also in UK and Italian laws.

The prevalence of facts over forms also applies with reference to the situation defined as a "silent partner." The *silent partner* is a person who invests some money in a partnership in return for profits, may participate or not in major decisions (but not in routine managerial decisions), and may even be unaware of what is happening in the business for a long period of time. American case law deems this person a partner, even if she/he is kept secret from third parties. In other words, the law does not distinguish between active (formal) and silent partners.

Who may have an interest in proving the presence of a silent partner? Creditors may have such an interest because in case the presence of a silent partner is proven, they may recover their claims also from her/his personal assets.

In the absence of any partnership agreement, all rules contained in the UPA shall be applied in case of any controversy among partners. They basically cover all kinds of situations. However, there might be some unfortunate unpredicted results as a consequence of such application.

Example

If one partner wants to withdraw from the partnership, she/he can insist that the other buy her/his interest or that the business be liquidated because this is the rule under the UPA, which provides that the termination of a partnership occurs at the will of any partner. This is the default rule. To amend this or, indeed, other rules contained in the UPA—which would apply automatically if there is no partnership agreement—parties may agree to draft a partnership agreement involving a lawyer, who may build tailor-made solutions for the partnership, taking into account the size of the business, the needs and preferences of the partners, etc. As UPA is made of mainly default rules, parties to a partnership agreement may decide to amend them as they wish.

What are the hot topics in drafting an agreement suitable for all? One issue, for example, is how partners shall share the profits and losses. One possibility is to share them in proportion to their contributions.

Example

If a partner contributes to the partnership's assets in the percentage of 10%, she/he will have the right to 10% of the profits and/or losses.

The optional solution could be to share them in a different proportion, disregarding their contributions, or, alternatively, to share them equally.

Another hot topic is the voting rule: unanimity or majority? Unanimity has the merit of involving all partners in any decision, but the drawback is that reaching an agreement can be difficult. Another important rule concerns the manner of counting votes. In this case, there are two possible models: one person/one vote or vote as a percentage of contributions.

Another clause can refer to the role of a "promoter," who is a person who may, in some cases, help find an investment opportunity and set a partnership and who may or not be a partner. Shall the promoter have a right to the distribution of profits? All these issues shall be settled in the partnership agreement; otherwise, UPA 1914 shall apply. We will come back to these rules as provided under the UPA in the following paragraphs.

3.2.2 The Reification Debate

A debate that has developed in the United States, the United Kingdom, and Italy concerns the legal nature of partnerships. This debate has been labeled in the United States as the reification debate. While corporations have a legal personality (which will explored in Section 4.1 below), it is not clear in all the jurisdictions we deal with whether a partnership is an entity, separate from its partners, even though it is not a legal person, or rather an aggregate of all the partners who are its members. Solutions may be different. UPA 1914 leaves the question unresolved, but UPA (in Section 201) states that a "partnership is an entity," even though some provisions reflect the aggregate theory. In England, Wales, and Northern Ireland, a partnership is not a legal person; under Scottish law, however, partnerships have a distinct legal personality. A consequence is that in the first case (England, Wales, and Northern Ireland), a partnership cannot become a member of another partnership (though the individual members may do so), while Scottish partnerships may become members of other partnerships.

The debate is not only theoretical because some practical consequences depend on this qualification. For example, if we qualify a partnership as an entity, all legal suits shall be brought by it or against it; if we deem it as an aggregate, the consequence is that all partners (collectively) shall be plaintiffs or defendants in a legal suit. Another example is taxation: if we adopt the entity theory, the partnership itself shall pay taxes and, in addition, also partners when profits are distributed to them (so-called double taxation), but if we adopt the aggregate theory, only partners shall be taxed when profits are distributed to them.

Therefore, the general question remains unresolved, even though, in certain issues, there are statutes and courts that resolve specific problems.

3.2.3 Fiduciary Obligations Among Partners

What are the legal duties among partners? There are no specific rules contained under the UPA. However, Section 2 is titled "Partner Accountable as a Fiduciary." In addition, American case law has established that there is a *fiduciary obligation* among parties. The concept is vague: it assumes fairness, honesty, and good faith in the relationship among partners. In this respect, we find general clauses *in all the jurisdictions* under examination. It is not worthy nor possible to make categories because there is a variety of endless differing situations. We can think of examples to try to understand what a partner's behavior compliant with the fiduciary obligation should be.

Example 1

Suppose a partnership is set up between Mary and Andrew. They are engaged in a real estate brokerage business (i.e., they earn money by acting as agents for others in the purchase/sale of real estate). One day, Andrew is sitting at his office, and a person enters and seeks to sell property of great value for sale. Can Andrew buy the property for himself to sell it, later on, at value and make the profit? Or shall he share the opportunity with Mary? We would certainly conclude that the opportunity shall be shared with Mary as Andrew got to know about it while performing his job, during his office hours. But what if Andrew learned of this opportunity during the weekend or during a party? Would this circumstance change the rule?

Example 2

Let us assume the business is exploration and drilling for oil and gas. The partnership is among Mary (active partner), Andrew, and Matthew (silent partners). Suppose that Mary finds oil in a certain land (X) that the partnership had purchased: she will obviously share the information and exploit the land with the other partners. But what is the rule in case Mary gets to know that the adjacent land to X (Y) is available for sale? Very likely, land Y will be rich in oil as well and may rise in value. Can she buy the adjacent land and exploit it by herself, or shall she share the opportunity with the partners?

There are no precise answers to these questions; it really depends on the type of relationship among the partners in each case and, of course, on the possible clauses in the partnership agreement contemplating certain situations and consequential conducts. A careful examination of all the facts and circumstances is fundamental before drawing a conclusion. As above mentioned, the concept of fiduciary obligation is vague and broad.

An important analysis of the meaning of fiduciary obligations in partnerships has been rendered by the famous judge, Benjamin Cardozo, in 1928. According to him, a fiduciary obligation is the "Duty of finest loyalty [. . .]. A trustee is held to something *stricter* than the morals of the market place. Not honesty alone [. . .] but the most sensitive honor [. . .]. Uncompromising rigidity [. . .]. For fiduciaries [. . .] level higher than that trodden by the crowd [is required]."[2] This language has been criticized as being too excessive; however, it has the potential capacity to affect the outcome of particular cases where evidence of intent is sparse.[3]

A leading case that deals with fiduciary obligations among partners is *Latta v. Kilbourn et al.*[4]

Facts In this case, the partnership was originally composed of Hall, Kirkendall, and Kilbourn (under the name "Hall, Kilbourn & Co.") and set up for the purpose of carrying on the business of real estate brokers (i.e., negotiating and making sales and purchases of real property for the account of others). Later on, Hall withdrew from the partnership, and Latta succeeded Hall's interest. So the partners were Latta and Kilbourn. It was a partnership in parol (i.e., no written agreement); there was no original capital contributed and no property. Another element to consider is that Kilbourn had no financial resources, while Latta was rich. For a few years, real estate was bought by each partner on his private account with no share of profits. By *special agreements*, they made certain special ventures: (1) they bought, on a joint account and on speculation, two parcels of land when Latta advanced money, and the

[2] In *Meinhard v. Salomon*, 249 N.Y. 458, 463–64, 164 N.E. 545, 546.

[3] Klein (2021), p. 75.

[4] 150 U.S. 524, 541, 14, S. Ct. 201, 207–208, 37 L.Ed. 1169 (1893).

title was in his name. (2) They also bought bonds and other securities on the partnership's books. (3) In some cases, profits were shared for property purchased and sold on behalf of others, but there was no share of losses. In 1871, a former employee of the partnership, Olmstead, was admitted as a partner. There was no written agreement and no change in business. The habit was to divide profits, at the end of each year, according to respective interests (3/8 + 3/8 + 2/8). Later on, there was a verbal agreement according to which "knowledge of any property that was offered for sale or any property that any of the members of the firm knew about, should be communicated to the firm, and, if they saw fit, and were in condition, they could buy it; and, if either member declined, the other two could, or, two declining, one could; but everything pertaining to real estate was to be for the benefit of the firm, and to be communicated to the firm" (please note that there was such a verbal agreement according to what was testified by Olmstead and Kilbourn, while Latta denied its existence). Subsequently, Latta and a third party, Stearns, engaged in *some joint purchases of real estate on speculation.* The other two partners knew about them and never opposed anything. The partnership was dissolved in 1877, and thereafter, Olmstead and Kilbourn sued Latta, claiming that he was accountable to the partnership for the profits ($45,000) made in joint purchases with Stearns. They also added that they had no knowledge about them until after the dissolution and that Latta had conducted them secretly. Latta denied that it was ever agreed, either in writing or by parol, that the partnership's business was to buy and sell real estate on the partnership's account and that at no time, in fact, did the partnership undertake to carry on such business. He also argued that the scope was rather that of *real-estate brokers* and that this business continued the same after Olmstead came into the firm as before and that it was so advertised to the world. He further denied that there was any agreement, either written or in parol, that all profits resulting from the operation in real estate by such firm, or any member thereof, should belong to the firm.

Principles of Law The District of Columbia decided: "The complainants are entitled to recover from said defendant *their full share*, viz. five-eighths of all profits realized by said defendant from said sales of real estate referred to in the pleadings and proof in this cause, made by said John Stearns and said defendant, with interest thereon from the time when the same were so realized." Why? According to the Court, Latta could not engage in purchases of real estate on his own account or in connection with others, except with the *consent of his partners*, without violating the duty and obligation that he owed to his firm, and even if the partnership did not include the business of buying and selling real estate on the partnership's account, still Latta could not employ the knowledge and information acquired in the course of the partnership business in respect to the real-estate market in making purchases or transactions for his own benefit. The Court proceeded on the basis of the following general principles: one partner cannot, directly or indirectly, use partnership assets for his own benefit; cannot, in conducting the business of a partnership, take any profit clandestinely for himself; cannot carry on the business of the partnership for his private advantage; cannot carry on another business in competition with the firm, thereby depriving it of the benefit of his time, skill, and fidelity, without being accountable to his copartners for any profit that may accrue to him therefrom; cannot be permitted to secure for himself that which is his duty to obtain, if at all, for the firm of which he is a member; and cannot avail himself of knowledge or information that may be properly regarded as the property of the partnership, in the sense that it is available or useful to the firm for any purpose within the scope of the partnership business. These general principles are nowadays known by the expression *"shall not" principles*, and they very clearly define what the contents of fiduciary obligations among partners are. However, on appeal, the US Supreme Court, while confirming the general "shall not" principles, stated that, in this case, those transactions entered into by Latta with Stearns were not within the scope of the business; therefore, there was no duty upon Latta toward his firm; he was not the agent of the firm. The proof affirmatively established that the partnership agreement did not extend to the business of buying and selling real estate either for investment or for speculation on the firm's account. It was just brokerage; appellees never testified to the contrary. Partners may traffic outside of the scope of the firm's business for their own benefit and advantage. Nor can it be properly said that Latta used any information that was partnership property so as to render him chargeable with the profits made therefrom. His knowledge of the real-estate market, or in respect of profitable investments therein, was not used in competition with the business of the firm nor in any manner so as to come within the scope of the firm's business. The cause was dismissed even though the "shall not" principles were confirmed and remain very important in US jurisdiction to understand the contents of the fiduciary obligations among partners.

3.2.4 Control

As explained above, the core issues embodied in partnership law in the three jurisdictions covered by this book are control, agency, and liability.

Control, which is the power to manage the partnership, i.e., to take all relevant decisions in order to carry on the business activity day by day, includes questions like how to carry on the business, how many employees to hire, whether to open new offices, how much to invest per year, how much to borrow from a bank, etc.

Section 18(e) UPA 1914 states that

> "*All partners* have equal rights in the management and conduct of the partnership business," and under Section 18(h) UPA 1914, "any difference arising as to ordinary matters connected with the partnership business may be decided by a majority of the partners."

Accordingly, all partners together have the right to participate in decisions and to express their vote. What is the *voting rule?* Since all partners shall express their votes, the voting rule is unanimity. With reference to ordinary (i.e., day-by-day) matters, if there is no agreement among all partners, as stated by Section 18 (h) above, the decision is taken by a majority of the partners. In other words, if unanimity cannot be reached, in order to make a decision, the majority rule applies, but this possibility merely refers to ordinary decisions. This is well explained in another provision, Section 18(h) UPA 1914.

Section 18(h) UPA 1914 states:

> No act in contravention of any agreement between the partners may be done rightfully without the consent of all partners.

In the new language of UPA 1997, Section 401(j) states:

> An act outside the ordinary course of business of a partnership and an amendment to the partnership agreement may be undertaken only with the consent of all the partners.

Therefore, the rule is that when dealing with ordinary decisions, in case unanimity cannot be reached, the majority rule applies. But if the act is outside the ordinary course of the business or the decision concerns an amendment to the partnership agreement, unanimity is required.

Example

Let us assume that the partnership agreement limits the scope of the partnership business (e.g., a restaurant activity) and that in the partnership agreement there is no rule to change the scope. What is the voting rule? The answer is unanimity. What happens if decisions are taken by the majority in violation of such a rule? The typical remedies that shall be asked before the courts are injunction (in which case the court stops the execution of the decision) and damages.

In case the majority rule applies, how is it counted? The rule is that of *one partner/one vote.*

All these rules can be altered because—as explained above—a major characteristic of partnership law is that of consisting of mainly default rules. Variations shall be inserted in the partnership agreement either when the partnership is set up or later; in the latter case, the amendment of the agreement requires consent by all partners. For example, a different control rule could consist of allocating powers to only a few partners (rather than to all of them); this model of control is defined as *representative government.* Partners who are allocated the representative government can decide by unanimity or majority, depending on the choice made by all partners in the partnership agreement.

Another variation can refer to the one partner/one vote rule; in this case, the alternative voting rule could be to count votes as the proportion of contributions (e.g., if a partner contributes 10% of the assets, her/his vote will count 10%).

3.2.5 Agency

What is the meaning of agency? Agency is the power to enter into legal relationships on behalf of the partnership and that binds the partnership itself. Any business activity to be carried out needs entering into contracts and other agreements, i.e. with suppliers, lenders, employees, etc. When a contract is signed by an agent, it binds the partnership, which becomes a party to the contract and shall bear all obligations arising from it. Who are agents in a partnership?

Section 9(1) UPA states:

> Each partner is an agent of the partnership for the purpose of its business.

The act of any partner within the scope of the business binds the partnership. Thus, each partner has the power to dispose of any or all assets of the partnership and even to dissipate them, exposing the other partners to personal liability. In other words, agency authority is an incident of status as partners; it need not be consciously conferred to them.[5] Being a partner automatically means being the agent of the partnership.

However, also Section 9(1) UPA is a default rule, and therefore, it can be amended in the partnership agreement. Agency powers may be conferred to just a few partners and not to each of them or to all partners jointly (in the latter case, this would mean that all partners shall sign all contracts). Another possibility is to limit agency power to a certain value of contracts entered into (e.g., $100,000). However, any limit inserted in the partnership agreement, that departs from the legislation, shall be notified to third parties who enter into contracts with the partnership in order to be enforced against them. Alternatively, knowledge of the agency limit by third parties shall be proven; otherwise, the contract binds the partnership anyhow.

In any case, as per Section 9(1) UPA, mentioned above, agency is allocated to each partner, but the limit is the *purpose of the business*. Therefore, in partnerships, the purpose of the business is very important because it stands as a perimeter of the agency power for each partner and also as a perimeter of the legal capacity of partnerships.

Example 1

Mary, Andrew, and Matthew are partners in a grocery store business. In the partnership agreement, there is a clause under which each partner is an agent of the partnership for acts up to a limit of $200. One day, Andrew decides to buy from Mr. Smith a new checkout costing $400.

Is the contract of sale between Andrew and Mr. Smith valid? Does it bind the partnership? According to Section 9(1) UPA, the answer is yes: the contract is valid

[5] Klein et al. (2010), p. 93.

because it is a purchase related to the business of the partnership and binds the partnership to Mr. Smith even though the value of the transaction exceeds the limit set in the partnership agreement. There are consequences for Andrew, who shall pay damages to the other partners for any losses suffered by them, but the contract is valid and binding. Why? Unless the limitation of power/authority was notified to Mr. Smith or it is proven that Mr. Smith knew about the limitation, the contract binds the partnership. The underlying reason is that the *good faith of third parties* is always protected. By contrast, if the third party knew about the limit in agency powers, the contract would not have any legal effects because Andrew had no such power/authority from the partnership for an act of this value. To explain the concept in different words, only acts outside the purpose of the business do not bind the partnership; other limits to agency powers may be enforced *vis-à-vis* third parties only if the third party was aware (further to notification or proof of knowledge) of this limitation.

There is an exception only with reference to the transfer of *real property* by partners: third parties are deemed to know any limitation to it if it is contained in a partnership statement filed in the appropriate state office (UPA (1997), Section 303 (e)).

Example 2
In the same partnership (operating a grocery store business), Andrew buys from Mr. Smith a machinery to produce clothes. Does the agreement bind the partnership? The answer is no because under Section 9(1), the agency powers of partners are limited to entering into contracts that are *related to the purpose* of the partnership: a machinery to produce clothes has nothing to do with the grocery store business. So the contract would produce no legal effects on the partnership.

3.2.6 Liability

In partnerships, each partner is potentially liable for the full amount of partnership debts.

The basic rule under both UPA 1914 and UPA 1997 is that liability is *prima facie* "joint and several." What is the meaning of this? The meaning of "joint" is that *all* partners are liable; the meaning of "several" is that a creditor may decide to ask for payment from only one of the partners (in other words, the creditor is not obliged to ask for payment of the claim from all partners simultaneously), and this partner shall pay the creditor; she/he will recover the balance of the claim paid from the other partners, proportionally to their amount, later on. For a creditor, it may be generally more convenient and simpler to claim payment from only one of the partners, especially when the creditor knows that one partner has enough resources to pay the entire amount of the debt.

Are partners liable just with assets contributed to the partnership or, additionally, also with their personal assets? Sooner or later, depending on each American state and courts, creditors are likely to be able to get *also partners' personal assets.*

May this rule be altered? What happens with reference to third parties? This rule may be altered in the sense that partners may agree that only some of them are liable for the partnership's debts and not all of them. This agreement, however, may be enforced upon third parties only if they are aware of it; otherwise, the principle of several liability does apply, and creditors may choose to claim payment from any of the partners.

Another possibility is to distinguish between liability for debts (that is, arising from contracts entered into by the partnership) and liability for damages (that is, arising from torts) in the sense that partners may agree to be jointly liable for debts, leaving individual liability for torts committed by single partners to them. In any case, if nothing is agreed upon by partners, the general principle is that partners are jointly and severally liable for debts and torts.

3.2.7 Termination

A partnership can be terminated at the will of all partners. However, if one partner dissociates from the partnership at any time, also in this case the partnership ends.

In the partnership agreement, there might be a *term*; the agreement on the term might also be tacit. If there is a term, the partnership cannot be terminated at will earlier on.

What if a partner, in breach of the agreement, wants to withdraw before the term? The others might liquidate the business or continue to operate it: the withdrawing partner is liable to pay for past debts and also for any damages the other partners may include. In any case, the remaining partners shall pay out the value of the withdrawing partner's interest. It is advisable to fix all these elements in advance, in the original partnership agreement: the contents of such clauses are called buyout/ continuation agreements.

If a partnership is terminated, the next step is the liquidation of all the partnership's assets, that is, the sale of the assets, in which a cash fund is produced to be used to pay off all debts. If there is any surplus left over, it is divided among the partners.

However, when a partnership is terminated, there are four possibilities: first, to shut down the business and sell all its assets (this is the liquidation mentioned above). In this case, any goodwill of the business is destroyed. Therefore, from a strictly economic viewpoint, this solution is not efficient. The second is to sell the assets as a going concern to an outsider. In this case, the goodwill would not be destroyed, but it might not be easy to find a purchaser. The third is to sell the assets as a going concern to a majority of the partners, in which case the goodwill would not be destroyed, and the minority partners would be bought out. The fourth is to sell the assets to minority partners as a going concern, in which case the goodwill would not be destroyed, but it might be expensive for minority partners to buy out the majority partners. In the latter three cases, all the partners shall agree on the solution.

3.2.8 Transferability of Interest

Can one of the partners transfer her/his interest in the partnership to a third party? In this case, the third party would become a new partner, replacing the transferor. The problem is that this transfer would mean a change in the partnership agreement: whether written or tacit, the agreement is entered into by specified parties, who are the partners. Any change among the partners is a change to the original agreement, and as for any of its clauses, it shall be approved unanimously by all the partners.

Is this a mandatory or a default rule? It is a default rule, and in the original agreement, partners may decide to provide for consent, instead of unanimity, merely by a majority of the partners or merely by the partners who have control or as partners may think fit.

3.2.9 Variations of Partnerships

In addition to sources of American law of partnerships, mentioned under Section 3.2 above, there are other sources of law that provide for special legal models of partnerships: limited partnerships (LPs), limited liability companies (LLCs), limited liability partnerships (LLPs), and mining partnerships. The partnerships dealt with so far are called general partnerships.

The *Uniform Limited Partnership Act*, dated 2001 and lastly amended in 2013, regulates limited partnerships (LPs), whereby there are one or more *general* partners and one or more *limited* partners. To general partners, the same rules examined so far apply; that is, they have full control and agency powers and are unlimitedly liable for the LP's debts. By contrast, limited partners do not control the business, do not have the power to act for the firm, and are not personally liable for the LP's debts; their liability is limited to their contribution to the LP. Limited partners have control merely over really major decisions, such as dissolution. But what happens if a limited partner does participate in a strategic decision? The consequence is that she/he will lose limited liability.

This type is especially used in the real estate business in the United States. The appealing aspect of LPs, compared to corporations (where all shareholders have limited liability), consists of tax considerations.

Limited liability companies (LLCs) are regulated under states' legislation. They are organized as a corporation but are treated like a partnership for income taxation. Therefore, limited liability is provided for investors (limited to the amount invested), and there is no double taxation on corporate income and investors' dividends because only corporate income is taxed. Control is allocated to all members; therefore, all of them can participate. It is formed like a corporation: legislation requires the drafting and filing of certain documents. Once formed, LLCs achieve the corporate characteristic of limited liability. The duration shall be no longer than 30 years. Members may withdraw at will by giving 6 months' notice. In most states, dissolution is caused by any member's death, withdrawal, bankruptcy, etc. But other members may continue the business if everybody agrees. The transfer of interest is free, but there is no right to participate in management on the part of the new member.

Limited liability partnerships (LLPs) are the newest type regulated by Section 306(c) of RUPA (and by states' legislation). It is a general partnership, but the liability of general partners is restricted: there is no personal liability for misconduct, negligence, and wrongful acts committed by other partners unless the negligence, misconduct, etc. has been committed under direct supervision or authorization by one or more partners, in which case all of them are liable. Unlimited liability merely refers to the LLP's debts; if it arises from the misbehavior of other partners, liability is limited to contribution. Therefore, according to this type, there is a sharp distinction between obligations for debts (i.e., obligations arising from contracts) and obligations for torts. However, some states (e.g., New York) provide limited liability for both obligations (those arising from contracts and torts) and require liability insurance coverage or the segregation of liquid assets in a special account (an escrow account) up to an amount so as to guarantee the payment of those obligations. This type is especially used by law or accounting firms that want to limit partners' liability that could arise from negligent advice or consultancy for which just one or more of them are, as a matter of fact, accountable.

Finally, *mining partnerships* are regulated by states' legislation. This type is used for mining ventures (including oil and gas). Rules have been developed by case law in consideration of the special nature of the business. It is a partnership, but interests are freely transferable; there is no dissolution at death or bankruptcy of one of the partners, the duration is defined by its scope, and there are narrower powers to bind the partnership according to agency powers.

3.3 Italian Partnership Law

The source of partnership law is the Civil Code. First and foremost, it must be pointed out that Italian law uses a single word, *società*, to describe any form of business association or organization with more than one member, thus encompassing the concepts of both partnership and company (but not sole proprietorship). Both partnerships (*società di persone*) and companies (*società di capitali*) are founded on contract and specifically on a contract of association (*contratto di società*).

Indeed, Article 2247 of the Civil Code provides as follows:

> By means of a contract of association (*società*) two or more persons contribute property or services in order to carry on an economic actitivity together with a view to sharing profits.

The object of any *contract of società* is the carrying on of an activity in common, that is, the creation of reciprocal rights and duties of collaboration in the management of an activity. The activity must be economic in the sense of being pursued with the view that income will exceed the expenditure, thereby generating a profit for the benefit of the members. Accordingly, there is no contract of *società* when the parties do not envisage a joint pursuit, i.e., the creation of rights and duties of collaboration. Neither is there a business association if the contract envisages solely the enjoyment of one or more things in common or if the contract provides that any excess revenue will be devolved for charitable purposes. Do no-profit organizations fall within the definition of partnership? No, because no-profit organizations do not pursue the aim of sharing profits among their members.

Partnerships (*società di persone*) are regulated by Articles 2251–2324 of the Civil Code. Partnerships do not enjoy a separate legal personality from that of their constituent members. The partners have, in principle, unlimited personal liability for the partnership's obligations, and hence, partnership creditors can enforce any claims against the partnership *and* the individual partners themselves. The relationship between the partnership and the partners and among the partners themselves is conditioned by *intuitus personae*, that is, reliance and reciprocal trust (or *affectio societatis*). This personal element represents the fundamental distinction between partnerships and companies.

The rules for partnerships contained in the Civil Code are essentially default rules; that is, they are of a supplementary nature in the sense that they apply to the extent that the partners have not agreed otherwise. This means that partners have an enormous degree of freedom in determining their relations with one another, save for some provisions that cannot be derogated from.

There are three types of partnerships:

1. Noncommercial partnership (*società semplice* (SS))
2. General partnership (la società in nome collettivo (SNC))
3. Limited partnership (la società in accomandita semplice (SAS))

The principal difference between a noncommercial partnership (SS) and the other two types of partnerships is that the former—as the name itself suggests—may not have commercial objects, i.e., may not engage in any of the activities listed, by way of example, in Article 2195 of the Civil Code. Therefore, a noncommercial partnership may have an agricultural purpose or may engage in activities characteristic of a small entrepreneur (the cultivation of land, small trade, crafts, etc.) or in any other activities provided they are not of a commercial nature (for example, a noncommercial partnership may engage in a professional activity as it is not considered commercial under Italian law). On the other hand, the other two types of partnerships are referred to as "commercial partnerships" in that they may have commercial objects and hence are subject to the same special rules envisaged for commercial entrepreneurs, termed as the "statute of the commercial entrepreneur" (see Section 2.5 above).

3.3.1 Italian vs American Law of Partnerships

If we want to compare American vs Italian law, the following propositions can be drawn:

1. Partnerships share the same economic function so far explained.
2. Possible contributions to become partners are alike: goods (of any kind), services, real property, receivables, etc.
3. Regulation is mainly made of default rules, and there are few mandatory rules.
4. We find the same importance of mutual trust, reliance, and personal characteristics, so-called *affectio societatis*. As a consequence, the transferability of interest is allowed just in case of unanimity (but this is a default rule, under Article 2252 cc, like under American law).
5. The same distinction between partnerships and joint tenancy (specified in Italy under Article 2248 of the Civil Code) does apply.
6. The debate about reification is common to both jurisdictions. The Italian Civil Code does not expressly state that partnerships are separate entities; however, legal authors agree that they are separate entities even though they are not legal persons. Some legal authors draw a distinction between SS (arguing it is not a separate entity) on one side and SNC/SAS (arguing they are separate entities) on the other side.

Under the Italian Civil Code, the distinction between commercial and noncommercial activities remains also with reference to partnerships: SS is not allowed to exercise commercial activities; it is not a commercial partnership, and therefore, it is not subject to special rules regulating commercial entrepreneurs. Only SNC and SAS are allowed to exercise commercial activities; they are also called *commercial partnerships*, subject to the same special rules regulating commercial entrepreneurs (see Section 2.5 above).

3.3.2 Società Semplice (SS)

SS is regulated by Article 2251 to Article 2290 cc to carry out, as explained, noncommercial activities. Provisions dealing with SS do apply also to SNC and SAS unless expressly derogated by the two parts of the Civil Code regulating SNC and SAS.

SS can be set up with or without formalities; however, if one of the contributions is real estate, a written form is required. Partnerships born as a course of action are called, by Italian case law (the Civil Code actually does not contemplate them), *società di fatto* (partnerships in fact). Case law also recognizes partnerships that are born without realizing it—*società apparente* (apparent partnerships)—if they appear as such to third parties. Silent partners (*soci occulti*) are relevant under Italian law and may be subject to winding up procedures (in case the partnership is a commercial partnership), together with all other partners.

Being a noncommercial partnership, SS is *not* subject to a winding up procedure, shall *not* register with the Registrar Office—general section—and shall *not* draft and keep balance sheets and other records. The Civil Code just requires a yearly report, but there is no provision regulating its accounting rules. In an SS, profits shall be automatically shared among partners after the yearly report's approval: they basically belong to partners directly and not to the entity. The latter rule shows that actually there is no such distinction between the partnership's assets and the partners' assets.

How should profits and losses be shared among partners? The rule is that there is a proportion between the contributions to SS and the profits/losses. But this is a default rule, and partners may amend it. There is a mandatory rule, however, on distribution: the Civil Code declares void an agreement under which one or more partners do not bear any loss nor share any profit (so-called "lion" agreement or lion's share). Apart from this prohibition, regulation on how to share profits and losses is left to the agreement among partners.

In SSs the default rule, under the Civil Code, is that *each partner* (that is, individually) is allocated *control* in the absence of any clause to the contrary in the partnership agreement (so-called *Amministrazione disgiuntiva*). The partnership agreement may, however, provide that control be entrusted to only one or more partners. The advantage of this model (*Amministrazione disgiuntiva*) is that decisions may be taken very quickly; in this respect, the model is efficient. However, the disadvantage is that partners shall bear the consequences of decisions taken by one of them without fully agreeing with them or even without being aware of them. However, under the Civil Code, if one partner (A) is aware that another partner (B) is willing to do something A does not like, A may *oppose* the decision. Further to this opposition, the decision is frozen, and all partners shall decide whether the decision can be carried out or not. In this case, what is the voting rule? According to the Civil Code, in all types of Italian partnerships, the *voting rule* is a majority, calculated in proportion to the share in profits, which, as seen above, is proportional to the contributions (Article 2257 cc). This is a default rule, but in the partnership agreement, a different voting rule can be agreed upon: for example, one partner/one vote.

In the agreement, partners may opt for a different model: the so-called *Amministrazione congiuntiva* (Article 2258 cc), in which case control is allocated jointly to *all partners*, who unanimously decide on any business act. The advantage here is that the decision is taken with the agreement of everybody; there is consent from everyone. But the disadvantages are that this process can be slow and unanimity is difficult to reach, with the risk of a deadlock. However, the Civil Code provides that in case of urgency, a single partner may make a decision if this is essential to avoid possible damage to the partnership.

Article 2258 cc provides for *additional variations* to the model of control to be stated in the agreement: control may be allocated to one or more partners (delegation/representative government), and in this case, the managing partners may decide by unanimity or by a majority (proportional to the share in profits). However, the Civil Code leaves flexibility to partners on the model of control to be decided in the partnership agreement.

Likewise, *each partner* is allocated *agency* powers on behalf of the partnership to the extent that the partners do not agree otherwise. The default rule is that agency follows the same rules as control: the partner with control is allocated agency powers (Article 2266). So if the SS adopts the *Amministrazione congiuntiva* (Article 2258) model, all partners shall jointly sign any contract to bind the SS. If the SS adopts the *Amministrazione disgiuntiva* model, each partner may, by herself/himself, bind the SS for any contract, etc.

However, in any case, agency powers are limited to the *scope of the business* carried out by each partnership. If the act is out of the scope of the business, the partnership is not bound to third parties.

All types of partnerships (SS, SNC, SAS) can allocate control and agency powers only to the partners; that is, control or agency powers may not be allocated to a *third party*. This principle has been inferred from a majority of legal authors and case law as the Civil Code does not expressly state any provision on the issue. However, there are a few case law that have argued for the opposite rule (i.e., control or agency powers also to third parties).

As mentioned above, the fundamental principle of any partnership is that the partners are personally as well as jointly and severally *liable* for the partnership's obligations (Article 2267), a principle that allows creditors to claim payments also from partners' personal assets (i.e., unlimited liability) if the partnership's assets are not enough. However, this principle is not absolute. Indeed, in SSs, some of the partners (but not the partners who have agency powers) may *limit* their liability for the partnership's debts toward third parties by an agreement; in this case, liability would be limited to the contributions. The agreement is enforceable to third parties if it has been properly notified to them or it is proven by the SS that they were aware of it.

Example

Three of the four partners in "X Partnership SS" limit their liability and notify such to a third party, Mr. Y. If Mr. Y concludes a contract with the SS through the partner (Mr. W) who has not limited his liability and who is an agent of the partnership, then in the event of a breach of contract by the partnership, Mr. Y may enforce his claim only against Mr. W's personal assets and/or against those who contributed to the partnership. He cannot enforce his claim against the personal assets of the other three partners who have limited their personal liability because such limitation has been notified to him.

As mentioned, partners who are agents shall always bear unlimited liability: this is a mandatory rule for all partnerships in Italian law, and under it, agents are always liable to third parties. This rule protects third parties that may rely upon the accountability of partners who deal with them on behalf of the partnership.

If creditors of an SS want to claim payment for the partnership's debt, shall they ask for payment from the SS first, or may they choose to ask from the partners? The

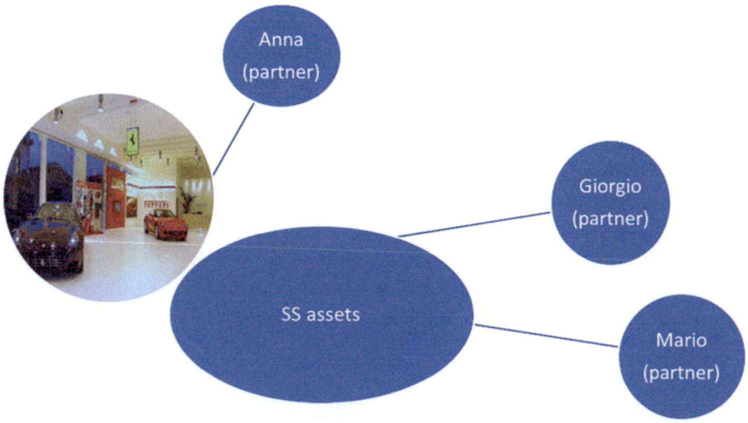

Fig. 3.1 A partner's personal creditor. Source: Author's own elaboration

rule for SS is basically that creditors may choose between the partnership's and the partners' personal assets (Article 2268 cc). However, if a partner is requested to pay for the partnership's debt, she/he may stop the claim *only if she/he identifies* and shows to the creditor the SS assets through which the creditor may be *"easily" satisfied*. "Easily" means promptly; in other words, assets shall be liquid or simply liquidated. For example, the banking account of the partnership is liquid, and shares/ debentures deposited in the name of the partnership are liquid as well; however, real estate is not liquid because selling it may require time. The rule according to which the creditors of an SS may choose between the partnership's and the partners' personal assets when asking for payment shows that the distinction between the partnership's and the partners' assets is not sharp, and therefore, the separation of SS as an entity from its partners is not strong. That is, with reference to the reification debate (see Section 3.2.2 above), considering the SS as a separate entity from its partners is not correct.

The Civil Code also regulates liability with reference to the *partner's personal creditor*, that is, the creditor who has a personal claim toward one of the partners, a claim that was born out of the business activity carried out by the partnership (see Fig. 3.1).

Example
Anna decides to buy a Ferrari car for her personal use from a car dealer. According to Article 2270 cc, a partner's personal creditor (in our example, the car dealer) may enforce her/his claims on the profits distributed to her/his debtor. If the debtor's assets are not enough to pay the claim, the personal creditor may ask, *at any time*, the SS to liquidate her/his debtor's interest in the partnership. From the date of the request, the SS must liquidate the interest

(continued)

within 3 months unless the termination of the partnership is decided. The SS has no discretion; if one of the partners' personal creditors makes a request for the liquidation of interest, the SS is obliged to liquidate the interest even though the consequence is the dissolution of the partnership (in case the contribution of that partner is essential for the business).

This is another rule that shows that the separation of an SS from its partners is very weak if personal decisions and acts of partners (such as, in the example made, the purchase of a Ferrari car) may interfere with the business activity.

3.3.3 Società in Nome Collettivo (SNC)

SNCs are regulated by Articles 2291–2312 cc. They are commercial partnerships, which means they may exercise any of the commercial activities and also non-commercial activities. In both cases, all special rules applying to commercial entrepreneurs (registration, balance sheets, etc.; see Section 2.5 above) do apply. However, winding up applies just in case the SNC carries out, in fact, commercial activities; all the other "commercial" rules always apply even if the activity carried out is not commercial.

Example
It is possible to set up an SNC with an agricultural scope. In this case, all rules applying to commercial entrepreneurs shall apply but for winding up.

An SNC may be set up *only with formalities*: a written form of the agreement and the partners' signature duly authorized by a notary are required or a public deed (by a notary).

With reference to *control* and *agency*, there are no differences with SSs: both are allocated by the Civil Code to each partner unless anything different is provided under the partnership agreement. However, any limitation (initial or subsequent) to agency powers shall be registered in the register of companies, to be enforced against third parties, who are deemed to know anything (but limited to what is registered), unless it is proven, by the partnership, that they were aware of some circumstances.

As for *liability*, all partners are jointly and severally liable for the partnership's debts, and liability is unlimited. An agreement limiting the liability of some partners may also be made in the context of an SNC, but in this instance, such an agreement has no validity *vis-à-vis* a third party. In other words, it is just an internal arrangement among the partners concerned. Therefore, a person who concludes a contract with a general partnership may enforce her/his claim against each and all the partners' personal assets and/or those vested in the partnership; *vis-à-vis* third parties, all partners are jointly and severally liable. Another difference with SS is

Fig. 3.2 Partners' liability in SNC. Source: Author's own elaboration

that in SNC, creditors must ask for payment from the partnership itself; only if the partnership's assets are not enough to satisfy the creditors' claim may they ask the partners to pay.

This is specified by Article 2304 cc, under which it is stated:

> Creditors, even during liquidation, shall not claim payment from partners *unless* they have preliminarily enforced the claim against the SNC assets.

It is a procedural prerequisite: in any legal action for payment by SNC creditors, the defendant shall, at first instance, be the SNC. Only if the creditors have proven that the assets are not enough to satisfy the claim may they sue each and all the partners. Interpreting the rule in light of the reification debate, it shows that an SNC is a separate entity from its partners (unlike an SS) (see Fig. 3.2).

The separation of the entity from the SNC partners' personal assets (differently from SS) is also confirmed by Article 2305 of the Civil Code on personal creditors.

Article 2305 of the Civil Code states:

> A partner's personal creditor may not ask SNC for liquidation of his debtor's interest until the partnership lasts.

Therefore, under this rule, it is clear that there is a sharp separation between the SNC's assets and its partners' assets: in no case may the personal creditors of a partner undermine the business activity by requiring the liquidation of interest, as happens with SSs. The partnership's debts and assets are fully and completely different from the partners' debts and assets.

Also, Article 2303 of the Civil Code on the distribution of profits shows another difference between SNCs and SSs that has implications with reference to the reification debate. According to the article, profits may be distributed to partners further to the approval of the balance sheet and only after having deducted the losses. That is, they must be *net profits*. There is no right for the partners of an SNC to share dividends unless they are declared as net profits by the partners who manage the partnership and unless these partners decide that they want to distribute the profits (rather than, for example, invest them). This is an additional rule showing the separation between the entity's assets and the partners' personal assets.

3.3.4 Società in Accomandita Semplice (SAS)

SAS is a *commercial partnership* with the consequences that the same rules applied to commercial entrepreneurs do apply. Like SNC, SAS may carry out a commercial or noncommercial activity.

This type is similar to an American LP; this is no surprise because SAS traces back its origins under Roman law, and this model influenced other jurisdictions (including US law through UK law). It is regulated by Articles 2313 to 2324 of the Civil Code.

There are general partners (*soci accomandatari*), with the right of control, agency powers, and unlimited liability for the partnership's obligations, and limited partners (*soci accomandanti*), having no right to control, no power to act on behalf of the firm, and no personal liability for the partnership's debts. Limited partners are expressly prohibited from exercising managerial or agency powers; if they contravene the prohibition, they become personally liable to third parties for all partnership's obligations and can be excluded from the partnership. The prohibition against limited partners, either managing or representing a partnership *vis-à-vis* third parties, is imposed by law, and a breach thereof—even by means of a single management action or a single case of representation—will render the limited partner in question personally as well as jointly and severally liable for all the partnership's obligations.

Example

If a limited partner (Mr. X) concludes a contract with Mr. Y on the partnership's behalf, then Mr. X is not only liable toward Mr. Y with reference to the specific contract concluded with him but is also liable for all other obligations of the partnership, regardless of whether such obligations have been assumed prior to or subsequent to the contract in question. The extension of all of a partnership's liabilities to a limited partner who breaches the prohibition against managing or representing the partnership, even by doing just a single action, can be justified by the fact that it is a sanction imposed by law in order to punish unwarranted interference by the limited partner in the partnership's affairs and also in order to undermine any intention of abusing this type of partnership to defraud creditors.

SAS may be set up only with *formalities* (like an SNC): a written form with the partners' signatures duly notarized or a public deed (by a notary).

With reference to SAS partners' *personal creditors*, the same provisions analyzed for SNC apply (with reference to both general partners and limited partners as these debts refer to personal relationships, and so the position of a partner in SAS is not relevant). With reference to *liability*, general creditors (like in SNC) shall enforce claims preliminarily over SAS assets, and in case they are not sufficient to repay the creditors, they may enforce the claims but only against the general partners.

3.3.5 Provisions Common to SS, SNC, and SAS

For all types of partnerships, a *duty of care* is required for partners who manage the partnership *vis-à-vis* the conduct of business of the partnership (Article 2260 of the Civil Code). The joint liability of the managing partners in the case of damage to the partnership is provided unless one partner is able to prove that she/he was not negligent. Damages are those suffered by the partnership's assets as a consequence of the breach of the duty of care. The standard of care is that of reasonableness: what a reasonable and prudent man would do in managing her/his own affairs; that is, no particular expertise is required for partnerships.

Partners who do not manage the partnership have the *right of being informed* by the managing partners as well as the right of consulting documents and receiving a report on the activity carried out.

The duty of care is not required by the Civil Code with reference to the relationship among partners. Unlike in the United States, there are no fiduciary obligations expressly provided under the Italian Civil Code among partners nor a duty of loyalty. However, it is generally assumed, by legal authors, that there is a general principle, under Italian law, *of good faith* (Article 1375 cc), which applies to all kinds of relationships and contracts, including partnerships and companies. It is not codified however, with reference to partnerships/companies, by addressing relationships among members. There is not much case law or discussion on breaches of good faith or loyalty among partners. The debate is much more developed and the standard much higher in American law with reference to fiduciary obligations (see Section 3.2.3 above).

Under the Civil Code, all types of partnerships can be *terminated* in the following cases:

1. Expiry of term
2. Fulfillment of the scope of business
3. At the will of all partners
4. If just one partner remains for at least 6 months with no other partner
5. Other causes that may be provided under the partnership agreement
6. Winding up (only for SNC and SAS, which are commercial partnerships)
7. Additionally for SAS, when merely general partners or merely limited partners remain for longer than 6 months

After termination, the *liquidation* of the partnership's assets starts upon the appointment of liquidators to generate cash funds and pay all debts; any surplus shall be shared among the partners, and any debt not covered by the partnership's assets shall be personally paid by the partners.

The Civil Code also provides for the *unilateral termination of partners*. This may occur in the case of:

1. Death of a partner: in this case, the other partners may choose whether to liquidate the interest to her/his heir(s) or to terminate the partnership or to carry on the partnership with the heir(s) (if they agree).
2. Withdrawal of a partner: this is available at any time if the partnership has no term (but giving 3 months' notice); if there is a term, withdrawing can be decided only for a "right cause" or for other reasons contemplated under the partnership agreement.
3. Exclusion of a partner for a serious breach of obligations provided under the law or under the partnership agreement or for any kind of disqualification (including crimes) or in case the partner's contribution perishes or the partner is not able to perform her/his promised services as a contribution—exclusion is voted by a majority of the partners (without counting the partner in question).
4. Declaration of bankruptcy of a partner: in this case, the exclusion is automatic; there is no vote.

Other causes may be included in the partnership agreement: even though some legal authors debate on the issue, a majority of legal authors believe that it is possible. For example, as an additional cause, the partnership agreement may provide for the breach of fiduciary obligations.

3.3.6 Professional Activity in Common

Article 10, subsection 3, of Law N. 183, dated 12 November 2011, introduced the STP (*società tra professionisti*), i.e., a partnership/company between professionals.

Is it a new type of partnership or company? No, it is not, because the mentioned provision just states that professionals can set up any type of partnership or company to carry out a professional activity following the provisions already contained in the Civil Code for those partnerships or companies. This new provision can be understood, considering that there used to be an old piece of legislation in force since the fascist era, dated 1939 (Law N. 1815/1939), according to which the exercise in common of a professional activity was prohibited. The reason was the clear distinction between professional and commercial activities permeating legislation since then and mentioned under Section 2.5 above; because they are different activities by nature, professionals were not allowed to use the same legal tools as did entrepreneurs. In 2011, the prohibition was abolished, but it is clear that a partnership or a company that undertakes a professional activity is not a commercial entrepreneur, and those provisions in force for commercial entrepreneurs (including winding up) do not apply.

3.4 UK Partnership Law: Sources of Law and Principles Common to the United States and Italy

The source of UK law of partnerships is *the Partnership Act 1890* (as amended).

According to its Section 1,

> A partnership is the relation which subsists between persons carrying on a business in common with a view of profit.

Likewise, under US and Italian laws, partners do not enjoy limited liability, partnerships are not granted a legal personality, and disclosure, registration, or other formalities are not required. Partnerships may be set up through an agreement or not; the agreement can be express or implied. A partnership can exist even without any of the partners being aware of the fact: what is required to have a partnership is the *factual nexus of carrying on a business in common with a view of profit*. There are no differences in this respect with both the United States and Italy. Similarly, all partners are liable and *even if they are not ostensible*: insofar it is proven that also not ostensible partners share the profits of a trading concern as a matter of fact, they are liable for the whole debt. The burden of proof is upon the creditors to show that there are not ostensible partners in addition to those who appear to third parties; creditors have such an interest, especially when there is a need to increase the number of assets from which to recover payments.

In UK practice, partnerships range from very large accounting and legal firms to very small owner-managed businesses. In terms of statistics, they are the same number as companies in the market. The inherent flexibility is the reason for their success. Like US and Italian legislation, the UK's Partnership Act 1890 imposes mainly *default rules*. Another reason for the success of partnerships in the UK is the tax treatment: partnerships are tax transparent, while companies are not.

Variation of the agreement is allowed with the consent of all the partners for mutual rights and duties. In particular, no change in the nature of the business is allowed unless all partners agree. Accordingly, the consent of all existing partners is required to introduce a person as a new partner in case a partner wants to transfer her/his own interest to a third party.

Similarly to US law (and unlike Italian law), courts have developed the principle of fiduciary duties among members themselves and from members to the partnership; the Partnership Act is silent on this topic.

3.4.1 Control, Agency, and Liability

According to Section 24(5) of the Partnership Act,

> "*Every* partner may take part in the management of the partnership business"; (8) "any difference arising as to *ordinary matters* connected with the partnership business may be decided *by a majority* of the partners."

That is, *control* belongs to each partner individually. In the case of a disagreement on ordinary matters, the decision shall be the one voted by the majority of the partners. In UK law, the voting rule is one person/one vote.

What happens in the case of a disagreement on extraordinary matters?

It is explained by the following paragraph of the same section:

> (8) . . . but no change may be made in the nature of the partnership business without the consent of all existing partners.

That is, when the disagreement refers to extraordinary matters, the voting rule is not a majority but unanimity. By extraordinary matters means the decisions out of the day-by-day business.

The legislation protects the partners' *right of information* on the partnership's affairs.

Section 25(4) states:

> (9) ". . . every partner may, when he thinks fit, have access to and inspect and copy any of [the books]."

Correspondingly, Section 28 states that partners who control the partnership have the duty to render true accounts and the full information of all things to any partner.

With reference to *agency powers*, under Section 5 of the Partnership Act,

> *Every partner* is an agent of the firm and his other partners *for the purpose of the business* of the partnership; and the acts of every partner who does any act for carrying on *in the usual way* business of the kind carried on by the firm of which he is a member bind the firm and his partners, unless the partner so acting has in fact no authority to act for the firm in the particular matter, <u>and</u> the person with whom he is dealing either knows that he has no authority, or does not know or believe him to be a partner.

Accordingly, agency belongs to each partner individually; agency powers are limited to acts that refer to the business of the partnership, carried out in the usual way. In case the partner has no authority (because agency powers have been limited for her/him) and enters into a contract with a third party, the partner does bind the partnership unless the third party she/he is dealing with is aware of the limitation of power or does not know or believe she/he is partner. In other words, the good faith of third parties is always protected.

The limitation of agency powers may concern specified partners (e.g., agency is allocated just to one or two partners but not to all of them—Section 5 above being a default rule) or may concern the type or value of the acts (e.g., agency may be allocated to every partner but for specified acts or may be allocated for acts up to a certain amount—in which case, for the specified acts or for those exceeding the identified amount, unanimity is required).

With reference to the *liability* of partners, Section 9 states:

> *Every partner* in a firm is liable jointly with the other partners, [and in Scotland severally also], for *all debts and obligations of the firm* incurred while he is a partner and after his death his estate is also severally liable in a due course of administration for such debts and obligations, so far as they remain unsatisfied. . . .

Liability expressly refers not only to debts but also to other obligations, that is, those that arise from wrongs or torts. It is interesting to note the difference between Scotland (where liability is also several) and the other UK jurisdictions—probably due to historical reasons. In all jurisdictions of UK however liability is not limited to contributions but includes also partners' personal assets and, after their death, their estate.

However, under Section 10, it is provided:

> Where, by *any wrongful act or omission of any partner* acting in the ordinary course of the business of the firm, or with the authority of his co-partners, loss or injury is caused to any person not being a partner in the firm, or any penalty is incurred, the *firm* is liable therefore to the same extent as the partner so acting or omitting to act.

This provision explains that the partnership is liable together with the partner who is liable for the wrongful act or omission; this is an example of vicarious liability (see Section 2.7 above).

3.4.2 Outgoing Partners and Dissolution

In UK partnerships, members may outgo in the case of:

1. Expulsion by all partners, unless the agreement expressly provides for a majority voting.
2. Retirement at will when the partnership has no fixed term—in this case, mere notice of the intention to the other partners is required.

The partnership itself may dissolve in the case of the following:

1. Expiration of the term (if fixed).
2. Termination of the venture or the undertaking.
3. If it is entered for an undefined time, by any partner giving notice of her/his intention to dissolve the partnership.

4. Death or bankruptcy of any partner, unless these events are differently regulated under the agreement.
5. The business becomes unlawful.
6. Upon the decision of the court.

Similarly to US and Italian laws, after dissolution, the liquidation of all assets to creditors starts, and any residual assets have to be shared among the partners.

3.4.3 Variations of Partnerships

The *Limited Partnerships Act*, dated 1907, regulates limited partnerships, whose characteristics include distinguishing between general and limited partners. Like in US and Italian laws, general partners have control, agency powers, and unlimited liability, while limited partners have no control and agency powers and enjoy limited liability. This type is nowadays used by venture capital, property investment vehicles, or agricultural tenancies.

Another type has been introduced by the *Limited Liability Partnerships Act*, 2000, and the Limited Liability Partnerships Regulations 2001: the former is just a short framework Act, while the latter sets out details, mainly incorporating, by reference, substantial parts of other Acts. Therefore, there is no easily accessible corpus of legislation available for potential users of this variation of partnership because the Regulations do not contain a comprehensive set of rules but cite other statutes. Despite the name, an LLP is not a modified form of partnership but a *modified form of company*. It was a response to the pressure for limited liability within a partnership relationship from professional firms and their threat to move offshore. Many of the provisions of the abovementioned legislation still bear the imprint of the original purpose, even though LLPs are available to all activities and not just to the regulated professions. LLP is a body corporate with a legal personality and limited liability: its members are not personally liable for its debts beyond their financial interests in the entity. It has an *unlimited capacity*, which means that agency powers are not limited to the purpose of the partnership (as generally occurs with reference to agency powers); this is a typical characteristic of companies, as will be analyzed under Section 4.1 infra. LLP is incorporated by registration with an incorporation document; it is subject to many of the accounting and disclosure requirements and other controls applicable to companies. However, there are no shareholders or share capital, neither directors nor specific requirements as to meetings and resolutions—unlike rules for companies. In the case of insolvency, an LLP is subject to winding up, and there are additional clawback provisions fixed in the agreement that may require members to make payments to creditors. We can say that externally, LLP is treated like a company, but internally, it may be run as members wish with no formal requirement in legislation for any written agreement. However, there are the same number of default rules as partnerships. The taxation is direct, the same as for partnerships. Transforming from a partnership into an LLP is tax neutral, whereas changing from a company into an LLP is not.

With reference to liability, Section 1(4) of the LLP Act states:

> The members of a limited liability partnership have such liability to contribute to its assets in the event of its being wound up as is provided by the Act.

Nothing else is said by the Act about the personal liability of members. This model was thought to protect all partners against liability for the negligence of one of them. But what about the personal liability of a negligent partner directly to her/his client, e.g., a negligent audit? The other partners are not liable, as stated under the mentioned provision. Is the negligent partner liable to the client? In some US states (e.g., Jersey), the statute makes it clear that personal liability for a partner's own negligence is unaffected by the existence of an LLP. But the UK Act does not have any such provision, and the government expressly rejected the idea of including one. There is a debate on this issue among authors. However, courts made reference to the Explanatory Notes to the LLP Bill, according to which it is specified that the limited liability of all partners *would not affect* the personal liability of the concerned negligent partner toward the client; this would preserve the professional ethos of personal responsibility. Therefore, the conclusion has to be that in LLPs, while partners are not liable for the negligent behavior of one of them, they are individually liable to their own clients in the case of negligent advice.

To sum up, an LLP is a hybrid creature but is based substantially on the corporate model, which represents the prevailing model over the partnership model. However, internally, default rules apply, the same as for partnerships; internal affairs are entirely a matter of agreement among the members, and if there is no agreement, partnership law does apply. Finally, there can be no LLP with one single member.

3.5 Composition of Partnerships: US, UK, Italy

Among the common characteristics of partnerships, it has been mentioned (see Section 3.1 above) the so-called *affectio societatis*, meaning the concept of mutual trust and reliance among partners. Can a partnership be consist of mere individuals (because of this element), or can it also be composed of entities?

According to Section 2 of UPA, the term "person," as a member of a partnership, is defined as "individuals, partnerships, corporations, and other associations."

Under American law, it is therefore clear, as specified by legislation, that members of a partnership can be individuals or any type of entity.

With reference to UK jurisdiction, the term person is meant to likewise include artificial as well as natural persons, hence an individual, a body corporate, or the trustee of a settlement.

In Italy, partnerships were originally conceived to consist merely of individuals: in the Civil Code, there are no provisions expressly referring to entities among those dealing with partnerships, and the Supreme Court, on more than one occasion, held that it was not legitimate for a company to be a partner in a partnership, even as a limited partner of a SAS. However, the provisions regulating companies in the Civil

Code were amended more recently (in 2003), to introduce the need for companies of the authorization by the general meeting of shareholders (Section 6.4.5 infra) in case a company wants to become a partner in a partnership. In other words, this new provision indirectly (i.e., not under the section of the Civil Code referring to partnerships, whose regulation was not changed, but under those addressing companies) recognized the possibility for companies (and, by analogy, other entities) to be members of a partnership.

To sum up, in the three jurisdictions, partnerships can be composed of both individuals and entities; the *affectio societatis*, meaning mutual trust and reliance, should therefore actually be interpreted and meant as an element not exclusive of individuals but one that can subsist also with reference to entities, that is in practice, with reference to the directors who manage the entities and with reference to the financial resources of those entities.

Reference

Klein WA, Coffee JC Jr, Partnoy F (2010) Business. Organization and Finance, Thomson Reuters, New York

Public Companies: Introduction and US Law 4

Contents

4.1 Common Features Across Jurisdictions

Nowadays, companies represent the most important legal form, in terms of capitalization, to carry out economic activity everywhere in the world. The big companies we know by name are all set as a public company or as a corporation (e.g., Nike, Apple, Barbour, Enel, Eni, etc.). Capitalism is represented, from a legal viewpoint, by companies. Why historically was this legal form so successful?

The original model, from which the modern public company originated in most of Europe and, subsequently, in the United States, was the East India Company, born in England in the seventeenth century: its shareholders had the power to appoint and remove, at any time, directors, and the shareholders were deemed the company's owners. At the same time, there was another model, the East India Dutch Company (*Oost-Indische Compagnie*), founded in 1602 and characterized, on the contrary, by

S. Bruno, *Foundations of Business and Company Law*,
https://doi.org/10.1007/978-3-031-71885-4_4

an oligarchic structure. In the English model, the East India Company, the general meeting made by all shareholders, and defined *generall Courte* was present. It was convened at least once a year in order to elect its governor (*Gournor*), its deputy (*Deputie*), and the 24 members of the Committee (*Comitties*), and the governor and the members of the Committee had to be shareholders.[1] The appointment had a duration of 1 year. In the general meeting of shareholders, the governor as well as the members of the Committee could be removed at any time and at will.[2] With reference to the East India Dutch Company, the Charter, granted to found the company, provided to allocate the government to a Council of Governors (*Bewindhebbers*) made of 60 members that, in turn, delegated the government to a smaller council made of 17 members.[3] In the East India Company, the shareholders, acting at a general shareholder's meeting, were vested with all the powers, including managerial powers, and could direct the actions of the governor and the Committee, who were obliged to execute their orders.[4] Each shareholder could exercise one vote (so-called *per capita* vote), regardless of the shares held. Therefore, the East India Company had a democratic structure in both respects: all powers belonged to the shareholders, and they enjoyed full equality in terms of voting rights.[5] On the contrary, in the East India Dutch Company, all powers were allocated to the governors, and shareholders had no possibility of either influencing their action or controlling the activity carried out by them.[6] Apart from the Netherlands, in the rest of Europe, the model of the East India Company was imported and regulated, firstly in France, by the *Code de Commerce*, dated 1807, and later by other jurisdictions in Europe, which adopted that Code. Later, in Great Britain, the cornerstone of company law was the Joint Stock Companies Act, dated 1844.

---

[1] It is interesting to observe that nowadays, in some American states, members of the board of directors are still required to hold at least one share of the company: O' Donnell (1952), p. 62.

[2] The Charter granted by Queen Elizabeth, founding the company, 31st December, 1600 (1893). The Register of Letters &c. of the Governour and Company of Merchants of London trading into the East Indies 1600–1619, Birdwood G and Foster W, London, pp. 163, 168–170.

[3] Gevurtz (2004), pp. 127–129.

[4] The Charter granted by Queen Elizabeth, founding the company, December 31, 1600, cit., p 175 s.; Clause 1 ff. (1621). In: The Lawes or Standing Orders of the East India Company, Allde E, London, pp. 1–5.

[5] The importance of the "*per capita* vote" was highlighted by Dunlavy (2006), p. 1365 who explained that the rule was indicative of the conception profoundly democratic of the company, meant as political institution and conceived as a community of equals as opposed to the opposite rule "one-share, one-vote" based on plutocracy that, later on, since the nineteenth century, became the common rule: "What is striking about these discussions of 'democracy' in the twentieth-century corporation is that plutocratic voting rights went unquestioned. They were implicitly accepted, one has to conclude, as just and natural and, indeed, democratic" (ibidem, p. 1365). However, a study on Charters, dated 1609, 1693, and 1698, shows that already at the beginning, the "*per capita* rule" had been changed in practice in order to attract more investments and therefore not because the conception of the company had changed: see Harris (2005), pp. 29, 46.

[6] Brunetti (1948), pp. 291–297; Galgano (2007), pp. 108–112.

Through companies, big amounts of capital could be collected from a large number of shareholders and invested to carry out important business ventures. For example, the East India Company was formed to trade with the Indian Ocean region, which was the most important business at that time; one century later, corporations were the driving forces behind the British Industrial Revolution, and in the nineteenth century, they also shaped the American Industrial Revolution. This legal form could overcome some of the disadvantages of the partnership form; most importantly, shareholders' liability was limited to the contributions made to the entity for the subscription of shares, with no prospect of personal liability, and therefore, shareholders were encouraged to make even large investments, looking forward to receiving a share in the profits but with a limited risk; on the other hand, the participation of shareholders in the company was made by equity, that is, shares, which could be freely transferred to third parties. Basically, corporations could raise capital from diverse sources, and this provided an important mechanism for savers, producers, and investors.

Companies worldwide are currently characterized by five common features: a legal personality, the limited liability of shareholders, transferable shares, delegated management under a board structure, and investor ownership.[7] In addition, regulation is mainly made by mandatory rules (differently from the law of partnerships).

As for *legal personality*, it entails several features. Companies have a "separate patrimony," that is, a pool of assets that are distinct from the other assets owned by the shareholders and of which the company itself, acting through its designated agents, is deemed in law as being the owner, with the right to use and dispose of them and make them available to its creditors. But the assets are unavailable to the personal creditors of the shareholders. This concept of "separate patrimony" has been defined as "entity shielding," which involves shielding the assets of the company from the creditors of the shareholders. In addition, companies are a "common counterparty" in relationships with third parties (suppliers, customers, employees, etc.) and in legal suits; therefore, they may enter into contracts (through directors who are vested with agency powers), sue third parties, and be sued by them. Moreover, having a legal personality also means that legislation provides for rules to govern the allocation of powers within the company and the procedures to regulate the internal organization of companies (i.e., formalities to convene the general meeting of shareholders or the meeting of the board of directors, etc.). In other words, internal organization in companies is not as flexible as in partnerships.

With reference to *limited liability*, a company's creditors, which have contractual claims against the company, are limited to making claims against assets that are held by the company itself and have no claim against the personal assets of the shareholders—contrarily to what happens in partnerships. However, shareholders are not exempt from liability because, to the extent of their contribution to the company's assets, they are proportionally liable for the company's debts (that is why the expression is that of *limited* liability and not of exclusion of liability).

[7] The identification of these characteristics is due to Kraakman et al. (2017), Chap. 1.

Limited liability is a form of "owner shielding," which is the converse of "entity shielding," which is identified above as a component of legal personality. While entity shielding protects the company's assets from the shareholders' personal creditors, limited liability protects the shareholders' personal assets from the claims of the company's creditors. These two elements, owner shielding and entity shielding, taken together set up a regime of *asset partitioning*, whereby a company's assets are pledged as a security against business creditors, while the personal assets of the shareholders are reserved for the shareholders' personal creditors.[8] However, limited liability refers to a company's obligations arising from contracts, i.e., it means a company's liability to creditors who have contractual claims (debts) against the corporation. In other words, limited liability, generally, does not include tortious liability (that is a company's obligations arising from torts).

While in partnerships (as seen above in Section 3.2.8), interests may be transferred only if all partners unanimously agree (even though this is a default rule), shares are *freely transferable*. This feature enhances the liquidity of shareholders' interests. The shares of public companies may be listed for trading on the securities exchanges. Therefore shareholders do not bear the risk of being stuck in the entity as they can exit by selling shares especially when corporations are listed on a stock exchange. However, jurisdictions also provide for some mechanisms to restrict transferability if the shareholders so agree in the articles of association or memorandum or separate agreements; restrictions of transferability however are prohibited if companies are listed on the securities exchanges.

Another feature of companies is that of vesting principal authority over corporate affairs in a *board of directors*, which is *delegated* with the task of making the most fundamental decisions. Boards of directors are generally separate from the company's managers. In certain cases, the principal authority can be vested in a sole director.

Finally, *shareholders are the "owners"* of the company in the sense that they have the right to oversee the company and the right to receive the company's net profits, which are generally proportional to the amount of their contribution to the company's assets. There may be different types of shareholders: individuals, institutional investors, hedge funds, long-term or short-term investors, private investors, or the state.

4.1.1 Why Companies and Corporations?

While British legislation uses the term "company", US legislation uses the term "corporation". The reason of this different terminology has historical roots. Since the eighteenth century, the internal organization of British-regulated companies, among which the East India Company, has influenced organizations all over the world, also because of the hegemony in trade of the British Empire, which lasted until the end of

[8] Kraakman et al. (2017), pp. 10–14.

the nineteenth century. However, in Great Britain, in order to react to some fraud and speculations and the consequential financial crises that occurred during the eighteenth century, the Bubble Act was enacted in 1720, introducing criminal sanctions and prohibiting the setting up of corporate bodies and the soliciting of subscriptions of freely tradable shares unless this privilege was granted by a law from the Parliament or by a Charter from the Crown. At that point, incorporation became very difficult to obtain, and in the market, new legal forms emerged in order to circumvent the Bubble Act, such as joint stock companies, which were *not* incorporated. Joint stock companies were technically trusts among parties or settlors (so-called *cestui que trust* and comparable to members of a company) and trustees chosen by the former and equivalent to directors. Settlors and trustees were mutually bound to comply with the provisions specified under the deed of settlement, which also regulated the disposal of the fund dedicated to the purpose of the trust; settlors subscribed to the stock of the fund and were also beneficiaries of the trust.[9] Through various disguising mechanisms, these subscribers could also transfer shares to third parties: for example, the transfer was conditional upon the approval by the trustees, or shares were fictitiously transferred first to another subscriber or to a trustee and then later to the real purchaser.[10] Later on, the Companies Act, enacted in 1862, prohibited to set up nonincorporated entities with over 20 members, and this new rule halted the use of trust to exercise large business activities. In the United States, after the revolution, there was no legislation similar to what was adopted in Great Britain. On the contrary, the various states granted incorporation without imposing compelling requirements or inquiring on the merits of the business venture; that is why "corporations" were widely spread, and there was no need to set up trusts.[11]

Despite this historical and legal distinction, in practice, the terms corporation and company have been and basically are interchangeable: for example (but there are several cases), the first entity ever set up in an American colony was defined, in the documents, as a "joint stock company" or a "business corporation," even though in its name the expression was "municipal corporation"; there were several entities that were called "companies," even when they were incorporated.[12]

[9]Cooke (1950), pp. 80–86; Maitland (1911), pp. 271, 279: "But there are two achievements of the trust which in social importance and juristic interest seem to eclipse all the rest. The trust has given us a liberal substitute for a law about personified institutions. The trust has given us a liberal supplement for a necessarily meagre law of corporations." Even though among practitioners at that time the distinction between incorporated entities, nonincorporated entities, joint stock companies, and partnerships was not so clear also because there were no precise rules regulating relationships among members and between members and third parties: see Holdsworth (1926), pp. 47–50.

[10]Cooke (1950), p. 110, and the various deeds mentioned by Dubois (1938), pp. 222–230.

[11]Cooke (1950), pp. 92–99. Even though also trusts were used along with corporations: Hansmann et al. (2005-2006) pp. 1335, 1394–1399; Maitland (1911), pp. 394–399.

[12]Davis (1917), vol. I, pp. 32–40, and vol. II, pp. 3–10.

4.2 Ownership Patterns in Financial Systems

By ownership pattern of a company means the composition of its share capital, that is, how ownership is split among small investors, controlling shareholders, and institutional investors. An ownership pattern characterizes the financial system of each jurisdiction and may influence *corporate governance* because it determines who controls the company in terms of economic power. Consequently, in order to balance the control power, it has to be established who has the incentive to gather information and to monitor the directors and the management. The ownership pattern may also affect the liquidity of the shares (i.e., the possibility to sell the shares and exit from the company). Depending on the ownership pattern, corporate governance rules may differ. By corporate governance means a set of company rules on management, control, monitoring, and supervisory powers—rules that change from one jurisdiction to another.

The most prominent pair of expressions to define financial systems in the world is *insider-outsider.*[13] Examples of *insider or bank-oriented financial systems* in Europe are Germany, Italy, and France. However, most financial systems in the world present this structure. The ownership pattern in insider financial systems is characterized by public companies that typically have a single strong shareholder (e.g., the state) or a family or group of shareholders that hold effective voting control and are called "controlling shareholders." Voting power lies in the *controlling shareholders*, who enjoy control premium. Capital markets are *illiquid*; cross holdings and interlocking directorates are common. This type of financial system is defined as "insider" because control (i.e., power to manage the company) derives from inside the corporation, namely, by the controlling shareholders through the directors they appoint. Management derives, directly or indirectly, from the majority shareholders, who appoint and control the directors. In this situation, the directors may tend to act in the interest of the controlling shareholders. Under these circumstances, good corporate governance rules should aim at balancing the power of the controlling shareholders and minimizing/preventing their agency problems (i.e., conflicts of interests, opportunistic behavior) by protecting minority shareholders and granting them special rights.

By contrast, in *outsider or market-oriented financial systems*, the control of most public companies is public; i.e., they belong to the market, ownership is generally dispersed and diluted, and there are typically no controlling shareholders. Examples of this model of financial system are the United Kingdom and the United States. The main characteristic of public companies belonging to this financial system is the separation between ownership and control: the shareholders being so many and with little holdings, they have no actual power or actual control over the directors and managers, who may therefore tend to freely run the company's affairs. This situation has been described by the notion of "collective action" problem that occurs whenever all individuals (in this case, shareholders), who would in theory better off by

[13] To expand these topics: Berglöf (1997), pp. 151–164; Franks and Mayer (1995), pp. 171–195.

cooperating (in this case by voting and exercising supervision over boards of directors), fail to do so because of conflicts of interests among themselves, or because they are too many and it is difficult to unite as group and coordinate their conduct (e.g., on how to vote), or because of "rational apathy" (that is, the indifference that one single shareholder may feel when it makes the reasonable assumption that its vote would not have any real influence on the final resolution of the general meeting of shareholders and, therefore, it is not worthy even spending time to read documents distributed before the general meeting or attending the meeting itself). These two elements described so far, collective action and the rational apathy, were, especially in the past and in the United States, overestimated and considered as the justification for allocating strong powers to boards of directors over shareholders as synonymous of efficiency: in other words, the reasoning was that, because of collective action and rational apathy, shareholders were not able to exercise their powers while directors were better suited to determine how to conduct the business and therefore owners (the shareholders) could almost blindly rely on directors to run the affairs, the so-called managerialist or white collar theory, with the consequence of shareholders' marginalization even with reference to the exercise of voting rights.[14] Originally, it was for Berle & Means, in 1932, to theorize the separation between ownership (belonging to the shareholders) and control (belonging to the directors/managers) and the consequential managerialism.[15] As explained, "shareholders who are diffuse and small in relation to the enterprise have limited capacity to instruct managers on what to do."[16] The corollary was the so-called Wall Street rule, according to which if shareholders are dissatisfied with the management, the most efficient tool they have is to exit from the corporation by selling their shares; activism (i.e., exercising voting rights) is discouraged as it is more efficient to sell shares; consequentially, passivity is encouraged. On one hand, the "Wall Street" rule should protect shareholders: they are not bound to be members of a company if they dislike its management; they vote with "their feet" (i.e., exiting the company). On the other hand, the exit option would, in theory, work as a potent weapon to improve corporate governance: directors are induced to run the corporation diligently; otherwise, shareholders might sell shares, whose price (if large percentages of holdings are sold) would consequently decline. However, at that time (beginning of the twentieth century), the ownership pattern of American corporations was quite different and much more diluted compared with the current situation: until the 1950s, 91% of shares in US-listed corporations were held, on average, by individuals.[17] But nowadays, institutional investors (which may offer both active and passive funds) own, on average, 80% of all the stocks in S&P 500 (that is, the index of the 500 biggest American-listed corporations); their representation in corporations'

[14] Roe (1994), pp. 6–12.

[15] Berle and Means (1932).

[16] Chandler (1977), pp. 491–493.

[17] Pinto (2011), pp. 20–21.

share capital skyrocketed since the 1990s.[18] A recent study shows that while in 1982–1984 the value-weighted average corporation (considering all listed companies) had 190 institutional shareholders owning 37% of the firm, in 2015–2017, institutional investors grew to 1106 owning 74% of corporations.[19] The issue is that with reference to institutional investors, conceiving the collective action problem or the rational apathy would not be accurate: institutional investors are big shareholders and have less difficulties in coordinating action among themselves; in addition, their "apathy" would not be justified, they being too big to be passive and to fail in actively exercising control over management, by voting in general meetings or through other forms of engagement with the directors and management. As a matter of fact, and to confirm the previous propositions, attendance and voting in general meetings have been increasing in proportion to the rise of institutional investors' share in corporations. Even the Wall Street rule does not work for them: each of them owning relevant stakes of shares, the exit strategy may not be feasible when, for example, share prices are lower than the original purchase price; in addition, it is not simple for owners of such relevant stakes in a company to reallocate resources. A recent study shows that a corporation's ownership is in fact surprisingly stable from 1 year to the next.[20]

Other characteristics of outsider financial systems are that stock markets are *liquid*, and there is a market for corporate control (i.e., the role of equity markets also consists of facilitating corporate takeovers). In this type of financial system, corporate governance rules should solve the agency problem, consisting in potential opportunistic behavior by the directors to the detriment of the shareholders, by strengthening disclosure (to make the market efficient), deregulating takeovers (deemed as an important deterrent for underperforming companies), and fostering legal actions (especially class actions) in the case of directors' misconduct. Other "gatekeepers" conceived to overcome agency problems are deemed to be auditors, rating agencies, authorities empowered with broad powers and functions (such as the Securities and Exchange Commission (SEC)), independent accountants or analysts and credit-rating agencies, investment banks, outside counsel, and also reputational motivations.

However, in comparing these two ownership patterns and consequential corporate governance rules, the conclusion drawn from more than one study is that no single form of ownership and governance "offers a panacea for the issues that confront all companies"; on the contrary, different ownership and governance requirements depend on various factors, such as the activities carried out, the markets in which they operate, and social and political conditions. Heterogeneity

[18] Greenspon (2019), at https://hbr.org/2019/02/how-big-a-problem-is-it-that-a-few-shareholders-own-stock-in-so-many-competing-companies. Accessed January 3, 2024.

[19] Lewellen and Lewellen (2022), at https://ssrn.com/abstract=4173466, p. 11. Accessed January 3, 2024.

[20] Lewellen and Lewellen (2022), p. 11.

rather than homogeneity is desirable, as well as experimentation; therefore on these issues, prescriptive regulation is unjustified.[21]

4.3 US Corporations: Sources of Law

Public companies in the United States are regulated by both federal and state laws. Federal law deals with the "external affairs" of corporations, while state law deals with the "internal affairs" of corporations. However, the distinction is not mandatory nor written in the Constitution. It is argued that, in particular during times of crisis or when a corporate issue is important, there is "competition" between federal and state regulation.[22]

Federal law regulates disclosure for publicly listed corporations with reference to voting, insider trading, takeovers, and class actions. The most important federal pieces of legislation for corporations are the Securities Act 1933 (the first-ever comprehensive legislation on listed corporations, issued soon after the Great Depression of 1929), the Securities and Exchange Act 1934 (which set up the Securities and Exchange Commission, the authority in charge of supervisory, regulatory, and sanctioning powers over listed corporations), the Sarbanes-Oxley Act 2002 (regulating financial recordkeeping and reporting, issued as a reaction to a number of major corporate and accounting scandals, including the Enron and WorldCom scandals), the Dodd-Frank Act 2010 (passed in response to the financial crisis of 2007–2008), and the New York Stock Exchange (NYSE) and National Association of Securities Dealers Automated Quotations (Nasdaq) Listing Rules (setting listing requirements to be admitted by these stock exchanges).

As for *state law*, each state passed its own legislation regulating internal affairs, such as rules on incorporation, the allocation of powers between directors and shareholders, distribution of dividends, directors' liability, defensive takeover tactics, tax rules, etc.—in other words, all subjects that do not refer to disclosure, securities, and listing rules are covered by state legislation. However, the American Bar Association adopted the Model Business Corporation Act (MBCA), firstly drafted in 1943 and periodically amended since then, and in 2016, a major revision was made. Being a "model," it is intended to provide states with the opportunity to adopt it; the MBCA has been adopted by 36 states.

Within US jurisdiction, those who want to set up a corporation may decide in which state to incorporate it. The general rule is that, regardless of where the corporation operates or where the shareholders reside or where the assets are located, *the law of the State of incorporation* applies to that corporation. That is why incorporators may choose among the 50 states, being free to operate everywhere. The question therefore is: which state to choose when incorporating a corporation in

[21] Franks and Mayer (2017), p. 44. Accessed January 3, 2024.

[22] Roe (2003), p. 588.

the United States? There are, as a matter of fact, some variations among states' legislation on, e.g., how to approve a merger (simple or supermajority of votes?), dividends, takeovers' defensive tactics, directors' liability, etc. A large majority of public corporations incorporate in Delaware (a tiny state), even though they establish headquarters in other locations.[23] Delaware does not follow the MBCA. What are the reasons for the *Delaware primacy*? One reason is that it has limited fees and tax obligations: competition among states to attract the largest number of incorporators (which means more revenues and business for the state) triggered a race played by providing various favorable rules. Actually, a debate among legal authors lies in whether the Delaware primacy is due to a race to the top (i.e., Delaware offers administrative expertise in corporate filings, specialized lawyers, and judges, as well as a comprehensive body of case law) or rather to the bottom (i.e., Delaware legislation actually offers more protection to directors against hostile takeovers or *vis-à-vis* shareholders or with reference to directors' liability, etc.—rules that are detrimental to shareholders' welfare).[24] It is worth noting that it is up to the founders (who will generally be the corporate directors) to decide the state of incorporation, and later on, it is still up to the directors to decide whether and where to reincorporate; therefore, since the decision depends upon the directors, it is convenient for them to choose the most favorable legislation for their own interests and position. For decades, Delaware has been the undisputed leader in the market for corporate law, but more recently, this superiority is being publicly challenged, in particular by Nevada and Texas. For example, Elon Musk, after having criticized Delaware courts, has decided to incorporate X, X.Ai, and Neuralink in Nevada and wants to move Tesla to Texas; Tripadvisor's controlling shareholders are attempting to reincorporate from Delaware to Nevada. In particular, Nevada's corporate law poses insurmountable obstacles to shareholder litigation. However, according to the Delaware Court of Chancery, reincorporation may constitute a self-dealing transaction, and at the same time, Tripadvisor's shareholders claim that reincorporation amounts to a breach of fiduciary duties. All these recent events show that, as a matter of fact, the market for corporate law puts pressure on states to relax their own corporate law and leads to the bottom American corporate law exposing it to a rising fragility.[25]

Other sources of corporate law, in addition to federal law, state legislation, and stock exchanges' regulations, are:

1. Case law: the United States belongs to the common law legal family; therefore, judgments are a source of law.

---

[23] According to the Delaware Division of Corporations, 67.8% of Fortune 500 companies are incorporated in Delaware, and 1.5 million corporations have registered in the state. For example, Apple is incorporated in Delaware (even if the headquarters are in California) and the same for Coca-Cola, Google, Ford, Amazon, etc.

[24] To expand on the two opposite views, see Romano (1993), pp. 87–93 (race to the top) and Roe (2993) (race to the bottom).

[25] As very well explained by Barzuza (2024).

2. Bylaws and certificate (or articles) of incorporation: these are corporate documents to be filed for purposes of incorporation and contain provisions that may amend state legislation (when rules are not mandatory) or regulate certain issues.

In order to identify corporate rules for US corporations, *all the mentioned sources* shall be considered.

Unlike most other jurisdictions in the world, the United States does not follow the model, originally adopted by the United Kingdom, for regulating public companies also through a code of corporate governance, that is, a set of principles/recommendations that companies may voluntarily comply with. Although several such codes do exist in the United States (issued by national associations, such as the Investors Stewardship Group and the National Association of Corporate Directors, or by research centers), none of them has been singled out, by legislators or stock exchanges, as "the US Corporate Governance Code," and none of them is subject to the "comply or explain" or the "apply and explain" rules, which are a key feature in UK and European jurisdictions, as we are going to see below (Section 5.1). In particular, the Corporate Governance Principles issued by the American Law Institute (ALI) are not comparable to the Corporate Governance Codes known by other jurisdictions: ALI Principles shall be deemed as guidance on certain specific topics (such as the duties of care and of loyalty and the business judgment rule). However, Section 406(c) of the Sarbanes-Oxley Act requires listed companies to adopt a code of conduct complying with the *code of ethics*, as regulated, which must promote the ethical handling of conflicts of interest, full and fair disclosure, and compliance with laws, rules, and regulations; it must be applied to all directors, officers, and employees. What happens in practice is therefore that listed corporations usually adopt their own Corporate Governance Guidelines.[26]

4.3.1 Ownership Pattern in the United States

As mentioned, the United States is an outsider financial system. However, the separation of ownership and control, identified by Berle and Means in 1932, is not valid anymore. Currently, shareholders are not so diluted; rational apathy is a much weaker argument. Notwithstanding, it may be deemed an outsider financial system because, on average, there is no stable single shareholder or group of shareholders controlling companies. Nowadays, institutional investors (public and private pension funds, insurance companies, foundations, hedge funds, universities, mutual funds, brokerage firms, banks, trust companies) own almost 74% of share capital on average, as explained in Section 4.2, while in 1950, 91% of shares were owned by

[26] See for example, Amazon, at https://ir.aboutamazon.com/corporate-governance/documents-and-charters/guidelines-on-significant-corporate-governance-issues/default.aspx, or Apple, at https://investor.apple.com/leadership-and-governance/default.aspx.

individuals (or retail investors). In particular, about 60% of shares are held in mutual funds, and this industry is now quite concentrated as 25 fund managers control 60% of all shares in the hands of investment institutions.[27] Therefore, the ownership pattern is actually a mix of *dispersed and concentrated shareholdings*.

Despite being an outsider financial system, an American public company is not exclusively composed of diluted shareholders and institutional investors: this model certainly represents the dominant model, but there are important corporations, such as The New York Times, Google, Tesla, Amazon, and Meta, where individuals (usually the cofounders) own a substantial amount of stocks. In recent years, however, ownership has become increasingly concentrated, especially in mid- and large-cap firms: a recent (notably comprehensive) study shows that in 2017, insiders (i.e., directors and managers) and affiliates (i.e., employees, companies belonging to the same group) together owned 5.2% of the value-weighted average firm, while the top five institutional shareholders owned 27.6% of shares, its top ten institutional shareholders owned 37.1% of shares, and its top 25 institutional shareholders owned 49.8% of shares (top shareholders vary across firms: most notably, small institutions match small firms and large institutions match large firms).[28]

For example, at the beginning of 2023, **Tesla's** share capital (listed on the Nasdaq market) was owned by 43.00% institutional investors, 14.39% Tesla insiders, and 42.61% retail investors (individuals). Elon Musk is counted among the Tesla insiders, and he is the largest individual Tesla shareholder, owning 13.43% of the company.[29] One should not be confused by the percentage held by institutional investors and erroneously think they may be deemed as controlling shareholders *per se* because those shares are held by many institutional investors (in Tesla, they are over 2800), and each of them owns a stake between less than 1% and almost 6%[30]). Even though, at least, the biggest investors may communicate with each other and coordinate on how they intend to vote or join coalitions, they do not *per se* control the company. Let us have a look at other examples. At the same period of time, **Amazon** share capital (listed on the Nasdaq market as well) was owned by 57.64% institutional investors, 9.80% insiders (of which 9.73% were owned by Jeff Bezos), and 32.56% retail investors.[31] **Pfizer**, listed on the New York Stock Exchange (NYSE), was owned by 67.68% institutional investors, 0.27% Pfizer insiders, and 32.05% retail investors.[32] **Apple**, listed on Nasdaq, was owned by 57.63% institutional investors, 0.11% Apple insiders, and 42.26% retail investors.[33] **Meta**, listed on Nasdaq, was owned by 60.93% institutional shareholders, 10.94% insiders, and 28.13% retail investors. Accel Ix LP is the largest individual Meta shareholder,

---

[27] Mazzuccato (2018), p. 144.

[28] Lewellen and Lewellen (2022), pp. 12–16.

[29] See https://www.wallstreetzen.com/stocks/us/nasdaq/tsla/ownership.

[30] See https://www.nasdaq.com/market-activity/stocks/tsla/institutional-holdings.

[31] See https://www.wallstreetzen.com/stocks/us/nasdaq/amzn/ownership.

[32] See https://www.wallstreetzen.com/stocks/us/nyse/pfe/ownership.

[33] See https://www.wallstreetzen.com/stocks/us/nasdaq/aapl/ownership.

owning shares representing 3.70% of the company.[34] As a final example, **Google**, listed on Nasdaq, was owned by 62.77% institutional shareholders, 3.35% Google insiders, and 33.88% retail investors. Brin Sergey is the largest individual Google shareholder, owning shares representing 2.86% of the company.[35]

Analyzing and comparing the data of the mentioned corporations, taken as examples for the US financial system, it is worth noting that Apple and Pfizer are those with the most diluted percentages of shares: in both companies, insiders or other individual investors do not reach 1%. In all the others, insiders reach substantial percentages of voting power—considering that the remainder of the share capital is quite dispersed. All companies show a substantial percentage of shares held by institutional investors. According to the American economic literature, some of these institutional investors may be deemed *block holders*, meaning investors with a stake conferring the ability and incentive to monitor and influence the management: for empirical purposes, block holders are identified with shareholders who own at least 5% of a company's share capital, even though this threshold is arbitrary since also by owning lower percentages, the definition for a block holder can be met.[36]

4.3.2 How to Set Up a Corporation: Types of Corporations

The process is very simple and inexpensive: incorporator(s) (at least one) sign(s) the certificate (or articles) of incorporation and draw(s) up the bylaws. The difference between these two corporate documents is that *bylaws* contain provisions on the business of the corporation, the conduct of its affairs, and the rights or powers of the shareholders, directors, and officers, while the *certificate of incorporation*, signed by all incorporators—with their names, addresses, etc.—contains the name and purpose of the company, the number of shares authorized for issue (i.e., the authorized share capital), the classes of shares, the name of agents, duration, limitation of the personal liability of directors, the corporation's rights or powers, and the rights or powers of the shareholders, directors, and officers. It can be noted that some of the contents between the two documents overlap, such as the rights and powers of the shareholders, directors, and officers: we will come back to this element in Section 4.3.3.

Incorporator(s) file(s) the articles usually with the Secretary of State, even online: upon acceptance of the articles by the state official, the corporation acquires *legal personality*. No minimum share capital to set up the corporation is required. Alternatively, instead of having one or more incorporators, corporations may be set up through promoters, who launch an initial public offering (IPO) to collect equity on the market. While incorporators deal with identified future shareholders, promoters deal with the general public of potential investors.

---

[34] See https://www.wallstreetzen.com/stocks/us/nasdaq/meta/ownership.

[35] See https://www.wallstreetzen.com/stocks/us/nasdaq/googl/ownership.

[36] Lewellen and Lewellen (2022), pp. 6–8.

Among corporations, we will refer to them as a "listed" or "publicly traded" corporation, in contrast to an "unlisted" corporation. A company's shares may be held by a small number of individuals whose interpersonal relationships are important to the management of the firm, in which case we refer to it as "closely held," as opposed to "widely held" corporations. It is common to categorize corporations as either "public" or "close" corporations, but not all companies with freely tradable shares, in fact, have widely held share ownership or are listed on securities exchanges. Conversely, it is common in some jurisdictions to find corporations whose shares are not freely tradable but that nonetheless have hundreds or thousands of shareholders and that, consequently, have little in common with a typical closely held corporation that has only a handful of shareholders, some or all of whom are from the same family.

The spectrum of corporations can be represented as:

1. *Closely held corporations*—with a small number of shareholders, with a modest economic scope, and where usually shareholders are also directors (therefore, there is no separation whatsoever of ownership and control)
2. *Intermediate corporations*—medium sized, in between the two most typical types; *start-up*—financed by a venture capital fund, for an initial public offering (IPO)
3. *Publicly held or public corporations*—widely dispersed, generally (but not necessarily) listed on stock exchanges (e.g. NYSE, Nasdaq)

Legislation provides for *common rules* for all the mentioned types; just for listed corporations, federal laws and stock exchanges' rules do additionally apply.

4.3.3 Allocation of Powers Between the General Meeting of Shareholders and the Board of Directors

The general meeting of shareholders elects the board of directors. Shareholders may be qualified as *residual claimants* because they have the right to claim all earnings after (that is why they are called "residual") the fixed claims of senior creditors and security holders, bondholders, other creditors, and preferred shareholders are paid. In other words, shareholders bear the risk of losing the investments made (but is limited to it).

In addition to the power to elect directors, the shareholders, in a *general meeting*, have the power to remove them with or without cause, unless the certificate of incorporation provides for removal only for cause—which is quite often the case, as a matter of fact. Other powers the shareholders can exercise at a general meeting are:

1. Amendments to the bylaws and the certificate of incorporation
2. Major structural changes (such as mergers, liquidation, and the sale of substantially all assets)
3. Most stock option plans

Moreover, the shareholders, at a general meeting of listed corporations, have been granted by the Dodd-Frank Wall Street Reform and Consumer Protection Act (Dodd-Frank), a federal legislation dated 2010 that required the SEC to adopt rules on this issue, the power to vote on executive compensation packages and "golden parachutes" during acquisitions or mergers.[37]

Shareholders' vote on executive compensation was introduced to ensure transparency usually with reference to excessive amounts of remuneration decided by the board of directors itself, particularly after 2008, when the country suffered from a devastating financial crisis; some authors presented evidence that executive pay arrangements, such as stock options, encouraged excessive risk-taking and short-termism, which ultimately had deleterious effects on the whole economy.[38] In particular, the *Walt Disney* facts that occurred during those years (see below, Section 4.3.8) were perceived as outrageous by public opinion. The Congress's reaction was the enactment of this rule called *say on pay*. With reference to "golden parachutes," the vote was meant to prevent any opportunistic behavior of directors who, facing a merger or a takeover proposal, might be tempted to advance it even if not in the interest of the company itself or of the shareholders but just because they receive large payments from the bidder in exchange of their resignation or removal in the new company after the merger or the takeover is successful (that is why they are called "golden parachutes", i.e. the large payment (golden) given as rescue (parachute). However, it has to be highlighted that shareholders' vote on executive compensation is an *advisory vote*; i.e., it is not binding on the board of directors, who may decide to disregard this vote; that is why it is called "say on pay." The procedure is that the proposal for a certain remuneration for directors starts from the Compensation Committee (made of a majority of independent directors) set within the Board of Directors (see below, Section 4.3.4) and is then approved by the board itself and thereafter submitted to the general meeting of shareholders for an advisory vote. In case the majority shareholders approve the proposal, there is no problem. If the majority shareholders cast negative votes, the board may nonetheless ignore that vote and confirm the remuneration proposed. However, it has to be highlighted that shareholders in several companies brought derivative suits against their directors, citing their "No" votes as evidence that there was no justification for those pays, that those votes "reflected the "independent business judgment" of the shareholders, and that the pay "was not in the interest of their firms"; the shareholders therefore attacked the compensation decisions as breaches of the duties of loyalty and good faith owed by corporate officials to their shareholders (see below on directors' duties in Section 4.3.6).[39] In other words, although the negative say-on-pay votes are not legally binding on the board of directors, they might nevertheless serve as evidence

---

[37] By the expression "golden parachute" means a large payment or other financial compensation guaranteed to directors and managers in case they are dismissed, further to a merger or a takeover.

[38] Bebchuk et al. (2010), pp. 257, 274–276.

[39] Morrissey (2013), pp. 1, 27–30, who examines several derivative actions brought in this direction.

that the directors have violated their duty to act in the best interest of the shareholders.

The power that is allocated to the *board of directors* is typically that of making ordinary business decisions, that is, deciding the day-by-day management of the company. In addition, all other powers that are not allocated to the shareholders at a general meeting belong to the board of directors: for example, the distribution of dividends, the buyback of shares, the adoption of defensive measures in case of takeovers, etc.

With reference to the powers allocated to the shareholders at a general meeting, it is worth pointing out that what is relevant is not only the power to make decisions by adopting a resolution but also the *power to initiate* corporate decisions to be adopted in a general meeting. While shareholders have the power to ask the board of directors to call a general meeting when the items are the election or removal of directors, there are limits on the shareholders' powers to initiate major corporate decisions. With reference to the power to amend the certificate of incorporation or to merge, reincorporate, or dissolve the company, under existing statutes, such decisions must be initiated by the board of directors.[40] In other words, all major corporate decisions can only be initiated by the directors. This means that *amendments to the certificate of incorporation* also require the *board of directors' approval* to be valid. Therefore, shareholders, by themselves, could *not* amend the certificate; only the board of directors may start the procedure to call the general meeting advancing the proposal to amend the certificate of incorporation. In other words, the board shall first adopt the proposed amendment in a board meeting, and after that, it shall call a shareholders' meeting, where the item of the agenda is to approve the amendment. Shareholders do not have the autonomous power to call a meeting to submit their own proposal/s to amend the certificate of incorporation. This means that, basically, shareholders have mere veto power over a proposal started by the directors. In addition, the certificate of incorporation is deemed a *primary* source of law, while the bylaws are a secondary source of law: therefore, the latter cannot modify, amend, repeal, or be in contrast with the former, and the shareholders are not allowed to limit the directors' powers in the bylaws unless the certificate of incorporation provides for such a limitation.

Since the allocation of powers between directors and shareholders is an internal matter, that is, a subject regulated by state legislation, it is interesting to have a look at some of the legislation that contains specificities with reference to the distinction between the certificate of incorporation and the bylaws in terms of the power to adopt their amendments.

[40] Bebchuk (2007), pp. 675, 681.

Examples
The *Model Business Corporation Act*, Section 10.20, states that "(b) A corporation's board of directors may amend or repeal the corporation's *bylaws*, unless: (1) The articles of incorporation [. . .] reserve that power exclusively to the shareholders in whole or in part."

Basically, according to this provision, the shareholders' power to amend or repeal the bylaws is subject to what is written in the articles of incorporation, which, as above explained, can be changed upon the directors' initiative; in other words, the shareholders' powers with reference to the bylaws is subject to what the directors decide. However, the articles of incorporation may reserve this power only to the shareholders.

Delaware Code, Section109

. . .Any corporation may, in its certificate of incorporation, confer the power to adopt, amend or repeal *bylaws* upon the directors . . . [In this case.] such power shall not divest the stockholders nor limit, their power to adopt, amend or repeal bylaws.

Under this statute, therefore, shareholders' power with reference to the bylaws cannot be completely divested from them, but the certificate of incorporation (whose contents depend on what the directors wish to provide for) may allocate this power *also* to the directors, in which case the consent of both, the shareholders and the directors, is required in order to adopt, amend, or repeal the bylaws, and the shareholders do not have an autonomous power for it (if so provided by the certificate of incorporation).

New York Business Corporation Law, Section 601

The initial bylaws . . . shall be adopted by its incorporators . . . Thereafter . . . bylaws may be adopted, amended or repealed by . . . shareholders . . .When so provided in the certificate of incorporation or a bylaw adopted by the shareholders, bylaws may *also* be adopted, amended or repealed by the board. . .

Similarly to the Delaware Code, the New York statute envisages the possibility that the certificate of incorporation or the bylaw might allocate the power also to the directors, which would mean that both shall vote.

To sum up, in terms of the allocation of powers between the shareholders and the directors, with reference to the power to adopt, amend, and repeal the bylaws, solutions can be different from one company to another since each certificate of incorporation might adopt a different rule. However, it is only under the MBCA that the articles of incorporation may reserve that power exclusively to the shareholders.

4.3.4 The Board of Directors Model

In all American corporations, the board model followed is the *one-tier board model*: the general meeting of shareholders elects the board of directors, including the chief executive officer (CEO). The CEO chooses the *officers*, who manage the day-by-day business; officers are especially present in publicly held corporations. The board of directors exercises supervisory control over the business also with reference to the management of officers. Among the directors, it is possible to distinguish, especially in publicly held corporations, between *inside and outside directors*: the former category is made of directors who are in charge of executive powers, that is, managerial powers (obviously, the CEO is one of them, but there might be other directors empowered with management); the latter refers to directors who do not have any managerial power.

Usually, listed corporations establish, within the board, *internal committees* generally made of independent directors (see below, Section 4.3.5 on independence). Typically, the internal committees are:

1. The Nominating Committee and Corporate Governance Committee: tasked with making recommendations to the board regarding the size, structure, and composition of the board and the committees
2. The Compensation Committee, which reviews the components and the amount of directors' and top managers' compensation annually and makes proposals to the board
3. The Audit Committee, which assists the board in monitoring financial statements and other financial information, determining compliance with disclosure requirements, identification of external auditors and oversight of their independence and qualification, etc.

However, each corporation may choose to set up additional or different internal committees (such as the Strategy Committee; the Diversity, Equity and Inclusion Committee; etc.) and to allocate tasks and functions, which are specified in the charters adopted for each Committee, as the board of directors thinks fit. This subject is completely left to the autonomy of corporations, and nothing is regulated even by a Corporate Governance Code, which—as mentioned above—is not present in American jurisdiction.

4.3.5 Directors' Qualification

Under the Stock Exchange Regulations by Nasdaq and the New York Stock Exchange, the majority of directors must be *independent*, and the audit, compensation, and nominating committees are required to be composed solely of independent directors. The function of independent directors is to increase the quality of board oversight over executive directors and the management. There are various definitions of independent directors, such as outside, disinterested, and not having a material relationship with the company that would impair their independence. The board has the responsibility to make an affirmative determination that no such relationship exists.

Nasdaq and NYSE Regulations provide a list of certain relationships that preclude a board from finding independence: they are objective measures that provide transparency to investors and facilitate a uniform application of the rules as well as ease of administration.

Rule 5605(a)(2) of Nasdaq Rules

Independent director means:

"a person other than an executive officer or employee of the company or other individual having a relationship which, in the opinion of the Company's board of directors, would interfere with the exercise of independent judgment in carrying out the responsibilities of a director."

In particular, the following persons shall not be considered independent: a director who has been employed or has accepted (directly or indirectly) compensation from the company in the past 3 years or who has a family member who has accepted such compensation or who is a family member of an individual who is or has been employed as an executive by the company in the past 3 years. Reference is also made to any parent or subsidiary of the company.[41]

NYSE Rule 303A.02

No director qualifies as "independent" unless the board of directors *affirmatively determines* that the director has no material relationship with the listed company (either directly or indirectly). It is explained that "it is not possible to anticipate, or explicitly to provide for, all circumstances that might signal potential conflicts of interest, or that might bear on the materiality of a director's relationship to a listed company."

Accordingly, it is best that boards making "independence" determinations broadly consider *all relevant facts and circumstances.* Material relationships can include "commercial, industrial, banking, consulting, legal, accounting, charitable and familial relationships, among others." Reference is made to employment or

[41] For the precise definition: Nasdaq Rulebook, Rule 5605 (a) (2), at https://listingcenter.nasdaq.com/rulebook/nasdaq/rules/nasdaq-5600-series.

compensation by the company within the last 3 years and to relationships with the external auditor.[42] However, in both cases (NYSE and Nasdaq Rules), it is specified that the concern *is independence from management*, and therefore, the ownership of even a significant amount of shares by itself does not bar independence. In addition, it can be noted that "social relationships," which can be much harder to define, are not specifically addressed, even though they can have a big impact on the director's ability to perform her/his duties.[43] In any case, it has to be highlighted that the final evaluation of independence is upon the board: that is, the board is the "judge of its own cause." In any case, no specific provisions under legislation or regulations precisely cover what the roles, functions, and powers of independent directors are. Their function of oversight is just assumed but nowhere specified or regulated; at the end of the day, absent any rule, independent directors just have an incentive based on reputation to effectively oversee executive directors and the management; conduct is left to personal ethics.

Only corporations listed on Nasdaq shall meet an additional qualification for directors, under Rule 5605(f), introduced in August 2021, that requires companies to have:

> at least two *diverse directors* (if directors are more than 5), including: one self-identified woman director; one director who self-identifies as an underrepresented minority *or* as LGBTQ+.

By underrepresented minority means someone who self-identifies as African American or Black, Hispanic or Latinx, Asian, Native American or Alaska Native, Native Hawaiian or Pacific Islander, or two or more races or ethnicities. By LGBTQ + is meant an individual who self-identifies as a lesbian, gay, bisexual, transgender, or a member of the queer community.[44] If a company does not satisfy both of these criteria, the company must *specify* the particular aspect(s) of board diversity that it fails to satisfy and provide the *reasons* why it does not have two diverse directors. Disclosure must be provided in advance of the company's annual meeting of shareholders in its proxy or information statement or on its website. On the other hand, companies with five or fewer board members will only need to have one diverse board member (or explain the absence of a diverse director). Nasdaq explains that while it will verify whether a company has provided an explanation as to why it does not have two diverse directors, it will not assess the merits of the explanation and that there is no right or wrong reason that a company may give for not having at least two diverse directors. The sanction is therefore provided just in case of lack of

[42] For the precise definition: NYSE Listed Company Manual, Rule 303A.02, https://nyse.wolterskluwer.cloud/listed-company-manual/09013e2c85c00744.

[43] Gramm (2016), p. 141, writes that, for example, years ago at Walt Disney, the CEO, Michael Eisner, had his personal lawyer, his architect, and the principal of his children's elementary school on the board of directors.

[44] For the precise definition: Nasdaq Rulebook, Rule 5605 (f), at https://listingcenter.nasdaq.com/rulebook/nasdaq/rules/nasdaq-5600-series.

disclosure on diversity, in which case Nasdaq will assign a phase-in and grace period, till delisting, in case the disclosure requirement is not satisfied.

4.3.6 Directors' Duties and Liabilities

According to American case law, directors and officers are traditionally deemed as *fiduciaries* to the corporation. Fiduciary duties include the duty of care and the duty of loyalty.

Under the *duty of care*, directors are required to perform duties with the care and diligence of a reasonable person in similar circumstances. A breach of the duty can amount to malfeasance (negligence or gross negligence) or nonfeasance (failure to act). It is worth mentioning the "Principles of Corporate Governance (comprehensive treatment of corporate law on the duties and responsibilities of directors and officers)," published by the American Law Institute, explaining the meaning of the duty of care.

ALI, Section 4.01(a)

A director or officer has a duty to the corporation to perform the director's or officer's functions:

1. in good faith,
2. *in a manner that he or she reasonably believes to be in the best interests of the corporation*, and
3. with the care that an ordinarily prudent person would reasonably be expected to exercise in a like position and under similar circumstances.

A fundamental concept to consider in understanding the contents of the duty of care is the *business judgment rule (BJR)*. This rules implies that directors are granted full discretion in taking managerial decisions. More precisely, this rule limits the questioning of business decisions, both by the courts (i.e., courts shall not examine substantive issues or merits) and by the shareholders. From a legal proceeding's viewpoint, it is a *rebuttable presumption* that the director has acted in good faith, in an informed manner, and in the best interest of the corporation as a whole, that is, a presumption that the duty of care standards have been met. Therefore, the *burden of proof* that these standards have not been met is upon the *shareholders*, who must show that there has been a breach, for example, that the directors were in bad faith or did not gather all material information or showed gross negligence or lack of reasonableness or prudence or did not follow the procedures required by law or the articles of association. In other words, under this rule, the *merits* of the decisions taken by the directors cannot be reviewed by the courts; what the courts can evaluate is whether the right *procedures* have been followed by the board. However, the business judgment rule can never be claimed in case of conflicts of interest, bad faith, or waste. In addition, pending hostile takeovers, the directors of the target company cannot claim the business judgment rule; rather, it is upon them to demonstrate that the transaction was inherently fair to the shareholders according to the so-called *modified business judgment rule*—a pattern that was established by the *Unocal* case (and therefore was called "Unocal test").[45]

The Principles of Corporate Governance by the American Law Institute so explain the meaning of the business judgment rule:

ALI § 4.01(c)

A director or officer who makes a business judgment in good faith fulfils the duty under this section if the director or officer:

1. is *not interested* in the subject of the business judgment;
2. is *informed* with respect to the subject of the business judgment to the extent that the director or officer reasonably believes is appropriate under the circumstances;
3. and *rationally believes* that the business judgment is in the *best interests of the corporation.*

As chancellor of the Delaware Court of Chancery William T. Allen stated, "The [business judgment] 'rule' in effect provides that where a director is independent and disinterested, there can be no liability for corporate loss, unless the facts are such that no person could possibly authorize such a transaction if he or she were attempting in good faith to meet their duty."

With reference to the *duty of loyalty*, directors must act *in good faith, in the best interest of the corporation as a whole.* They shall show an undivided loyalty to the corporation. This duty can be breached in the case of an actual intent to harm the corporation or an intentional dereliction of duty and a conscious disregard for one's responsibilities. Typical examples are transactions with a conflict of interest whenever one or more directors aim at pursuing a personal over a corporate interest. Unlike the evaluation of the duty of care, with reference to the duty of loyalty, courts have the power to scrutinize transactions to determine fairness. The *burden of proof is upon directors* to show that a transaction has been fair, that the right process has been followed, and that the substance is correct. In other words, more judicial involvement and scrutiny are allowed than in the duty of care cases. The so-called entire fairness test shall be shown by the directors to prove fair process and fair dealing. Usually, especially in listed corporations, independent internal committees are appointed within the board to decide on transactions; their presence testifies to the adoption of a fair process.

Comparing the burden of proof between the duty of care and the duty of loyalty, the difference is that while with the former the business judgment rule is a safe harbor and therefore the burden of proving the breach is upon the plaintiff (i.e.,

[45] *Unocal Corp. v. Mesa Petroleum Co.*, 492 A.2d 946 (Del. 1985).

shareholders), with the latter, courts have the power to scrutinize the transactions to determine fairness, and therefore, the burden of proof is reversed upon the defendants (i.e., directors on fairness, process, substance).

In the case of a breach of the directors' duties, the plaintiffs have either of the following two possible legal actions to pursue: class action or a derivative suit.

Class actions may be brought in the case of *direct harm* to the shareholders (or, indeed, other investors or third parties), that is, harm that directly damages the personal assets of the shareholders (or other classes), and it is not the consequence of the damage suffered by the corporation's assets, which actually may not be involved at all. The mechanism provided for class actions actually fosters litigation as those who suffer the same kind of damage within a specified period of time—damage caused by the same party—are automatically the plaintiffs in the class action against that party—unless they opt out. In addition, under American law, contingent fees between the plaintiffs and their lawyers are lawful; therefore, lawyers receive a percentage of the monetary amount that their clients receive if and when they win or settle the case. Moreover, each party pays its own litigation costs and does not have to pay the litigation costs of the counterparty if the case is lost. These two rules work as an incentive in terms of litigation as plaintiffs do not bear any risk when evaluating whether to start a legal action against directors: plaintiffs shall pay legal costs only if they win the case and just for themselves; in other words, they have nothing to lose in deciding whether to start a legal action. However, with reference to securities class actions in stock markets (and therefore for listed corporations), the federal law, *Private Securities Litigation Act*, dated 1995, shall be considered. It provides for easier burden of proof for investors-plaintiffs with reference to monetary damages, but it also sets limits to stem the filing of frivolous lawsuits. To start a class action on behalf of investors, the plaintiff must be an "appropriate representative"; that is, it must hold a certain threshold of shares or other securities, and judges have the authority to determine the plaintiffs; as a matter of fact, only a large institutional investor may act as a representative on behalf of the class of investors. In addition, the amount of evidence that the plaintiffs are required to present before filing a case has been increased.

Derivative suits can be filed by one or more shareholders in case the harm is suffered by the corporation's assets and, indirectly, as a reflection of the devaluation of the assets' value, it impacts the share value and therefore impacts the shareholders who own those shares. While securities class actions are regulated by federal legislation, derivative suits are regulated by states. There is no threshold specified to start a derivative suit. However, there are strict procedural rules for shareholders, who shall: be record owners throughout the litigation, verify the truth and bring evidence on more facts, have adequate representation and own shares at the moment of wrongdoing, and exhaust all intracorporate remedies. In certain states, also the approval of the derivative suit by the board of directors (despite the fact that they are the defendants...) is required.

4.3.7 What Is the Interest of the Company?

Under both the duty of care and the duty of loyalty, reference is made to what a director reasonably believes to be *in the best interests of the corporation.* This means acting in the best interests of which constituencies? The principle is explained as acting in the interest of *the corporation as a whole*. But a corporation is an abstract, legal person, so it is important to better qualify the expression "corporation as a whole."

Delaware case law predominantly makes reference *to shareholders*: much attention has been given traditionally to the *Revlon* case, according to which the board must attempt to achieve *the highest value reasonably available to shareholders.*[46] However, the principle is limited to situations where the board has determined to sell control of the target company pending a hostile takeover: in that situation, the fiduciary duty consists of maximizing immediate stockholder value by securing the highest available price. Indeed, most fiduciary duty litigation has so far arisen in the context of mergers or other extraordinary transactions, but around the same time that *Revlon* was decided, the Delaware Supreme Court decided two other cases: *Unocal*[47] and *Household*,[48] which affirmed the board's ability to consider *all stakeholders* in using a poison pill to defend against a takeover—clearly confining *Revlon* to sale-of-control situations.[49] During that era of hostile takeovers (the 1980s and the 1990s), a majority of states (i.e., 32) have passed "constituency" or "stakeholder" statutes that *allow* corporate directors to consider nonshareholder interests when making business decisions without incurring liabilities.[50] Stakeholderism was introduced by these states as the basis for anti-takeover legislation, even though a consideration of nonshareholder constituencies was allowed for any decision.[51] These statutes, however, *do not limit directors' powers*; rather, they give them broader discretion to operate without a challenge; they are *merely permissive* by providing that directors "may," at their discretion, include a consideration of nonshareholder constituencies (i.e., the interests of employees, customers, suppliers, and sometimes creditors, local communities, or even the whole economy or nation) in their decision-making.[52] Some statutes even specify that the rule does not require directors to give priority to any particular interests over others.[53]

---

[46] *Revlon, Inc. v. MacAndrews & Forbes Holdings, Inc.*, 506 A.2d 173 (Del. 1986).

[47] *Unocal Corp. v. Mesa Petroleum Co.*, cit.

[48] *Moran v. Household International, Inc.*, 500 A.2d 1346 (Del. 1985).

[49] Lipton et al. (2019), https://corpgov.law.harvard.edu/2019/08/24/stakeholder-governance-and-the-fiduciary-duties-of-directors/.

[50] The Committee on Corp. Laws of the Am. Bar Ass'n (1990). The Committee quantifies the number of states in "at least twenty-five states," but it is dated 1990; the number is now higher—32, as specified in the text.

[51] Barzuza (2009), p. 1973.

[52] Macey (2020), p. 25.

[53] Bebchuk and Tallarita (2020), pp. 91, 106–110; they also explain that only one state, Connecticut, originally *obligated* directors to consider the interests of stakeholders but that later, in 2010, the statute was changed into a merely permissive approach (ibidem, nt. 53).

Apart from specific situations, such as mergers and extraordinary transactions, for several decades, shareholder primacy had been the principle assumed in the United States, mainly based on theories by Friedman and the Chicago School.[54] Therefore, directors were deemed to manage corporations aiming at maximizing value for shareholders (so-called *shareholder value*).

Ultimately, the Delaware conception of shareholder wealth maximation prevailed, and, as explained in *Re Trados*, directors owe fiduciary duties "to the corporation and its shareholders"; that is, the "stockholders' best interest must always, within legal limits, be the end. Other constituencies may be considered only instrumentally to advance that end."[55]

Or, to use the words of a classical leading case, *Dodge v. Ford Motor Co.*, "A business corporation is organized and carried on primarily for the profit of the stockholders. The powers of the directors are to be employed for that end. The discretion of directors is to be exercised in the choice of means to attain that end, and does not extend to a change in the end itself, to the reduction of profits, or to the non-distribution of profits among stockholders in order to devote them to other purposes."[56]

With reference to the duty of loyalty, it has been affirmed that actions are taken "in the good faith belief that they are in the best interest of the corporation and its stakeholders."[57] Also, it is concluded that "a clear-eyed look at the law of corporations in Delaware reveals that, within the limits of their discretion, directors must make *stockholder welfare their sole end*" and that Delaware corporations can consider stakeholder interests "only as a means of promoting stockholder welfare."[58]

It has been rightly said that "at the turn of 21st century shareholder primacy was still the dominant view" in the United States.[59] However, some authors argue that directors should focus on the maximization not of shareholders' value but, more broadly, of their *welfare*, given that shareholders (in particular institutional investors) are showing to care more than about just money.[60]

Recently, there has been concern about the negative consequences of shareholder primacy and short-termism, and more attention, on the other end, is given to

---

[54] Friedman (1970), p. 32, criticized those in the business community who maintained that private enterprises had a mission to promote desirable social ends. In Fama and Jensen (1983), pp. 301, 302, the starting point was the conception of organizations (including corporations) as a nexus of contracts; the central contracts specify the residual claimants (i.e., shareholders) and the decision-making body (i.e., the board of directors); therefore, relationship shall be between these two parties.

[55] *In re Trados Inc. S'holder Litig.*, 73 A.3d 17, 36–37 (Del. Ch. 2013) (Vice Chancellor Travis Laster).

[56] *Dodge v. Ford Motor Co.*, 170 N.W. 668, 684 (Mich. 1919).

[57] Strine et al. (2009), p. 3.

[58] Strine (2015), pp. 761, 768. It is to be noted that Strine LE, Jr., is a judge at the Delaware Supreme Court.

[59] Bebchuk and Tallarita (2020), pp. 99–102.

[60] Hart and Zingales (2022).

sustainability issues and long term. In 2019, the Business Roundtable, the American Association composed of the CEOs of major American corporations, announced a revision of its corporate purpose and signed the following statement:

While each of our individual companies serves *its own corporate purpose*, we share a fundamental commitment to all of our stakeholders: 1. Clients (delivering value to customers); 2. Employees (investing in them); 3. Suppliers (dealing fairly and ethically with them); 4. Community (supporting them); 5. Shareholders (generating long term value).

The declaration was made by 187 CEOs heading companies with an aggregate capitalization exceeding $13 trillion, which could have had a great impact on society and capitalism but, instead, was proven to have resulted in a largely "rhetorical public relations move rather than an actual change in corporate strategy."[61] However, the Council of Institutional Investors responded to this statement by the Business Roundtable, disagreeing with it as it places shareholders at last and refers to shareholders simply as providers of capital rather than as owners, clarifying that "to achieve long-term shareholder value, it is critical to respect stakeholders, but also to have clear accountability to company owners." On the other hand, "accountability to everyone means accountability to no one."[62] More recently, though, the so-called ESG debate (that is, debate on environmental, social, and governance issues, which together are identified as categories of stakeholders) has gone from a good governance topic to a hotly contested element within the US political landscape, it being under attack from various sides, and the United States has been going down quite differently from Europe in this respect, as we are going to analyze in Section 6.2.

4.3.8 Leading Cases on Directors' Duties: Applications of the Business Judgment Rule

Smith v. Van Gorkom[63]

Van Gorkom, chairman and CEO of Trans Union, a publicly traded company, was suggested by the company's chief financial officer (CFO) to undergo a leveraged buyout to an entity, which could offset a large tax credit. The suggestion came without any substantial research on price, but the CFO and the CEO thought that a $50–60 share price (on stock currently valued at a high of $39½) would be acceptable. Earlier on, in July 1980, the board of directors met to discuss the 5-year forecast, but there was *no mention* of a sale of the company. On September 13, Van Gorkom met Pritzker, a corporate takeover specialist; before the meeting, Van Gorkom did not consult the company's CFO nor the board of directors and asked the CFO not to let anyone know

(continued)

[61] Bebchuk and Tallarita (2020), pp. 111–115 prove, among other aspects, that none of the companies amended its corporate governance guidelines further to the statement or were affected by it or, strikingly, endorsed shareholder primacy in its guidelines; the study also shows that about 70% of the companies that signed the statement were incorporated in Delaware, where the approach, as explained above, is toward shareholder primacy.

[62] Council of Institutional Investors Responds to Business Roundtable Statement on Corporate Purpose, Washington, D.C., August 19, 2019.

[63] *Smith vs. Van Gorkom*, 488 A.2d 858 (Del. 1985).

and to calculate the feasibility of $55 per share sale. Van Gorkom also agreed with Pritzker not to solicit other bids and not to provide proprietary information to others. On September 18, Pritzker offered a cash-out merger at $55 per share; the deadline to accept was September 21. Van Gorkom called special management and board of directors' meetings for the following day, or on September 19, without specifying the agenda. At the management meeting, no documentation was provided; the reaction was negative. At the board of directors meeting, there was a 20-minute oral presentation—with no written documents; the proposed merger agreement was delivered, but there was no time to review it in advance. Van Gorkom did not explain how he arrived at $55. The board decided positively after a meeting lasting for 2 h. The shareholders sued the board of directors for breach of the duty of care. The issues of the legal action were:

1. Did the directors act with due care in deciding on the proposed cash-out merger?
2. If the merger was not the product of informed business judgment, did the board act with gross negligence?
3. Were the directors fully informed?

Even though there was actually a premium over the market price ($38 versus $55) for shares and no evidence of an interest by Van Gorkom in the transaction, the decision was that the business judgment rule did not apply in that case as it *presumes directors act on an informed basis, in good faith, and in the company's best interests*. A decision is informed if directors consider *all information* reasonably available before making the decision. In this case, the directors approved the merger without (i) determining Van Gorkom's role in the decision-making process, (ii) being informed about the determination of the price, and (iii) having prior notice of the decision. This could not be considered an informed decision, and the directors were held to have breached the duty of care.

It has to be outlined that, further to this decision, the Delaware Code was amended in 1985 as follows:

DGCL §102(b)(7)

It allowed (and still allows) to insert in the certificate of incorporation):

"A provision eliminating or limiting the personal liability of a director to the corporation or its stockholders for monetary damages for breach of fiduciary duty as a director, provided that such provision shall not eliminate or limit the liability of a director: (i) For any breach of the *director's duty of loyalty* to the corporation or its stockholders; (ii) for acts or omissions *not in good faith or which involve intentional misconduct or a knowing violation of law*; .... or (iv) for any transaction from which the director derived an *improper personal benefit*".

Further to this provision inserted in the Delaware Code, 90% of Delaware corporations have amended their certificates of incorporation to adopt this "exculpatory clause" and limit directors' liability. In other words, the principles held by *Smith v. Van Gorkom* could not apply anymore if the company included this clause in its certificate. This immediate reaction by the Parliament of Delaware to amend its Code also sheds some additional light on the race to the top versus the race to the bottom debate with reference to the competition among states, in favor of the latter thesis (see Section 4.3 above).

In Re Walt Disney Derivative Litigation[64]

Disney's president, Mr. Wells, died in a helicopter crash in 1994. Eisner, the CEO, stepped in but had to undergo heart surgery 3 months later, so the board of directors decided to appoint a new president, Mr. Ovitz. Ovitz and Eisner, old friends, entered into a letter agreement outlining the terms of employment: a 5-year term with a generous severance package, subject to approval from the Disney compensation committee and the board of directors. The compensation committee met for 1 h but was not provided with a draft of Ovitz's agreement; it was informed that negotiations would continue. The committee approved the agreement, without requesting to review the final document, and granted authority to accept the final conditions. The board of directors then met; there was minimal discussion, and Ovitz was appointed, leaving the final negotiations to Eisner. After 14 months, Disney wanted to terminate employment with Ovitz; Eisner and another director were involved and agreed to the no-fault termination of Ovitz, recognizing *over $140 million* to Ovitz as per the agreement; there was, at that stage, very little involvement of the board of directors. The shareholders brought an action against the board of directors, claiming a *breach of fiduciary duties and/or waste*. The issues of the legal action were:

1 Did the Disney directors breach their fiduciary duties to the shareholders and/or commit waste by entering into/terminating employment agreement with Ovitz, which included a termination provision allowing for $140 million in severance payments after just 14 months of employment?

2 Was there a conscious and intentional disregard by the directors of their responsibilities concerning material corporate decisions?

According to the Court of Appeal, there was no breach of fiduciary duty as the law *presumes* that in making a business decision, directors act on an informed basis, in good faith, and with the honest belief that the action was in the best interest of the company. This presumption can be rebutted if the plaintiff shows that the directors breached the duty of care or loyalty or acted in bad faith. If this is shown, the burden shifts to the directors to demonstrate that their actions were fair to the corporation and the shareholders. Therefore, the decision was as follows: "As I will explain [. . .] there are many aspects of defendants' conduct that fell significantly short of the best practices of ideal corporate governance. [. . .] But Delaware law does not—indeed, and the common law cannot—hold fiduciaries liable for a failure to comply with the aspirational ideal of best practices [. . .]." "The redress for failures that arise from faithful management must come from the markets, through the action of shareholders and the free flow of capital, and not from this Court. Should the Court apportion liability based on the ultimate outcome of decisions taken in good faith [. . .] decision-makers would necessarily take decisions that minimize risk, not maximize value."

In other words, the Court of Appeal held that the procedure followed was not the best practice but that there was no breach of fiduciary duties or bad faith. The compensation committee met twice to consider the information, and the directors were fully informed. No lack of good faith was shown. There was no waste because the directors did not give away irrationally corporate assets. The business judgment rule principle was affirmed because otherwise, so the Court held, directors would abstain from making risky decisions, therefore minimizing the value of the company.

4.3.9 The General Meeting of Shareholders

The first question to be posed is whether the general meeting of shareholders (meant as a meeting where all shareholders participate in person or by proxy) is mandatory.

[64] *In re Walt Disney Derivative Litigation*, **907 A 2d 693 (2005)**.

All states permit special meetings and action by *written consent* (that is, with no real meeting), though default rules may vary. However, for listed corporations, the general meeting of shareholders is mandatory.

The procedural rules on the functioning of the general meeting are found in the bylaws. They concern issues of notice, quorum, voting mechanisms, record date, etc. In other words, there are no general provisions in states' legislation on these aspects, which are left to the corporations' choice. Generally, the agenda of the *annual* general meeting is fixed by the board of directors. As for *special meetings* (i.e., meetings additional to the annual general meeting), the Delaware General Corporation Law (DGCL), Section 211(d), allows the *board* to call them, while the MBCA, Section 7.02, allows the board *or 10% of shareholders* to call them. Shareholders have *the right to request* the board to convene a general meeting only if the items of the agenda are the *election and removal* of directors. In all other cases, the shareholders have no such right under legislation. However, courts have developed a shareholder voting right through the calling of special meetings as a *right of expression*, but such resolutions are *advisory, not binding*. The leading case is *Auer v. Dressel.*[65]

Auer v. Dressel

In this case, a special meeting was requested, in writing, by preferred stockholders reaching 55%. The items of the meeting concerned amendments to the bylaws on the following: (A) voting upon a resolution endorsing the administration of petitioner Joseph L. Auer, who had been removed as president by the directors, and demanding that he be reinstated as president; (B) voting upon a proposal to amend the charter and bylaws to provide that vacancies on the board of directors arising from the removal of a director by the stockholders or by the resignation of a director against whom charges have been preferred may be filled, for the unexpired term, by the stockholders only of the class theretofore represented by the director so removed or so resigned; (C) voting upon a proposal that the stockholders hear certain charges referred, in the requests, against four of the directors and determine whether the conduct of such directors or any of them was inimical to the corporation and, if so, to vote upon their removal and vote for the election of their successors; and (D) voting upon a proposal to amend the bylaws so as to provide that half of the total number of directors in office and, in any event, not less than one third of the whole authorized number of directors constitute a quorum of the directors.

The bylaws of the company, Section 2 of Article I, stated: "It shall be the *duty* of President to call a special meeting whenever requested in writing so to do, by stockholders owning a majority of the capital stock entitled to vote at such meeting." The president claimed that he had no knowledge or information sufficient to form a belief as to who stockholding was who signed the requests. Was the president's claim true? There was evidence that for ten days, he had signatures before him. In addition, the request was rejected on the ground that none of the purposes was "proper" for such a meeting according to the president. The petitioners asked for an order to call a special meeting before the Court of Appeals. The issues examined were:

1 Did the president have discretion in deciding whether to call the special meeting?

2 As ruled by the Court of Appeals, "There was no discretion in this corporate officer as to whether or not to call a meeting when a demand therefor was put before him by owners of the required number of shares."

3 Can officers ignore such requests?

The Court of Appeals held: "The important right of stockholders to have such meetings called will

(continued)

[65] *Auer v. Dressel*, 306 N.Y. 427, 118 N.E.2d 590 (1954).

be of little practical value if corporate management can ignore the requests, force the stockholders to commence legal proceedings, and then, by purely formal denials, put the stockholders to lengthy and expensive litigation, to establish facts as to stockholdings which are peculiarly within the knowledge of the corporate officers."
Were the purposes "proper?"
The Court stated that no reason appears as to why they were not. Despite that, it is to be noted that the obvious purpose of the meeting was (since 11 directors, of whom were class A stockholders, more than a majority of whom joined in this petition, elected nine and the common stockholders elected two) to hear the charges against four of the class A directors, to remove them if the charges are proven, to amend the bylaws so that the successor directors can be elected by the class A stockholders, and, further, to amend the bylaws so that an effective quorum of directors will be made up of no fewer than half of the directors in office and no fewer than one third of the whole authorized number of directors. In other words, the class A stockholders asked to call a special meeting to be heard on their disproval of management decisions, to elect and remove directors, and to amend the bylaws. However, the Court decided that "The stockholders, by expressing their approval of Mr. Auer's conduct as president and their demand that he be put back in that office, will not be able, directly, to effect that change in officers, *but there is nothing invalid in their so expressing themselves*" and stated that "the stockholders who are empowered to elect directors have the *inherent power* to remove them for cause" ("It would be preposterous to leave the real owners of the corporate property at the mercy of their agents, and the law has not done so"). Therefore, the order to call a special meeting was affirmed.

In addition to the right developed further to *Auer v. Dressel*, a company's bylaws may provide for shareholders' right to call special meetings. However, as a matter of fact, only 64% of the bylaws of corporations belonging to the S&P 500 index do provide for such a right but require high thresholds: for example, Amazon requires 30% of share capital to ask for a special meeting; the most generous companies require 20%.

4.3.9.1 Shareholders' Proposals for Listed Corporations

With reference to the shareholders of listed companies, their request to call a special meeting or to add an item to the agenda if the general meeting of shareholders has already been convened, is regulated by *Rule 14a-8 of the Code of Federal Regulations*, as amended in 2022. First of all, only a single shareholder (*no aggregation of multiple shareholders is allowed*) holding $2000 of the company's stock for at least 3 years, or $15,000 for at least 2 years, or $25,000 for at least 1 year may submit the request. The shareholder must file with management, 120 days before the date, a proxy statement and the proposal may not exceed 500 words and must not run afoul of subject matter restrictions. A proposing shareholder shall declare (by a written statement) that it is able to meet with the company (in person or via teleconference) and that it is available to discuss the proposal with the company. No multiple proposals under different names or through different representatives are allowed. In order to resubmit a proposal that was previously filed, in the past 5 years, various minimum thresholds are required: 5% in favor of the votes cast if previously voted on once; 15% in favor of the votes cast if previously voted on twice; or 25% in favor of the votes cast if previously voted on three or more times.

If a proposal is filed, the board of directors has thirteen grounds for excluding proposals (14a-8(i)), the most important of which are: if it is improper under state law ((i)(1)): or, relates to a matter of ordinary business ((i)(7)); or, relates to a matter $<5\%$ of business ((i)(5)); or, conflicts with a company's proposal ((i)(9)). The burden is on the company to demonstrate that one of the grounds occurs for exclusion. Generally, proposals refer to: amendments of bylaws, change of policy on certain issues (recently: on diversity, climate change, sustainability), voting mechanism, request of special reports, special committees etc.

It has to be highlighted that if the proposal is accepted and the special meeting is convened or the item is added to the agenda, the resolution approved by majority of shareholders *is just an* ***advisory vote*** *which is not binding for the board of directors* who are therefore legitimate to disregard that decision.

Examples of Shareholders' Proposals Under Rule 14a-8 of the Code of Federal Regulations

In Apple Proxy Statement 2022, the shareholders submitted six proposals, each one followed by a supporting statement from the shareholders, but for all of them, the board of directors delivered a statement in opposition to the proposal and recommended to vote "Against."[66] The proposals are as follows:

(a) The "Shareholders request our Board of Directors take steps necessary to amend our articles of incorporation and, if necessary, bylaws (including presenting such amendments to shareholders for approval) to become a Social Purpose Corporation and to adopt specific social purposes such as (A) benefitting (1) the corporation's employees, suppliers, customers, and creditors; (2) the community and society; and (3) the environment, and (B) exercising reasonable care to ensure that the Company's operations do not impose social and environmental costs that materially contribute to the degradation or destruction of important social and environmental systems."
(b) The "Shareholders request the Board of Directors revise the Company's Transparency Reports to provide clear explanations of the number and categories of app removals from the app store, in response to or in anticipation of government requests, that may reasonably be expected to limit freedom of expression or access to information. Such revision may exclude proprietary or legally privileged information."
(c) The "Shareholders ask the Board of Directors to oversee the preparation of a report, at reasonable cost and omitting confidential and proprietary information, on the extent to which Apple's policies and procedures effectively protect workers in its supply chain from forced labour, including the extent to which Apple has identified suppliers and sub-suppliers

(continued)

[66] https://www.sec.gov/Archives/edgar/data/320193/000119312522003583/d222670ddef14a.htm, p. 72 ff.

that are at significant risk for forced labour violations, the number of suppliers against which Apple has taken corrective action due to such violations, and the availability and use of grievance mechanisms to compensate affected workers. The report should be posted to Apple's website."

(d) The "Shareholders request Apple report on median pay gaps across race and gender, including associated policy, reputational, competitive, and operational risks, and risks related to recruiting and retaining diverse talent. The report should be prepared at reasonable cost, omitting proprietary information, litigation strategy and legal compliance information."

(e) The "Shareholders urge the Board of Directors to oversee a third-party audit analysing the adverse impact of Apple's policies and practices on the civil rights of company stakeholders, above and beyond legal and regulatory matters, and to provide recommendations for improving the company's civil rights impact. Input from civil rights organizations, employees, and customers should be considered in determining the specific matters to be analysed. A report on the audit, prepared at reasonable cost and omitting confidential or proprietary information, should be publicly disclosed on Apple's website."

(f) The "Shareholders of Apple Inc. ("Apple") ask that the Board of Directors prepare a public report assessing the potential risks to the company associated with its use of concealment clauses in the context of harassment, discrimination and other unlawful acts. The report should be prepared at reasonable cost and omit proprietary and personal information."

All the abovementioned shareholders' proposals were not approved by the majority shareholders but for the proposal under lett. (e).

Amazon Proxy Statement 2019

The shareholders filed 12 proposals, all followed by supporting statements from the shareholders, and the board of directors (like at Apple) recommended to vote "Against":[67]

(a) The "Shareholders request that Amazon.com, Inc. issue an annual report, at reasonable cost and omitting proprietary information, on the environmental and social impacts of food waste generated from the company's operations, given the significant impact that food waste has on societal risk from climate change and hunger."

(b) "The Shareholders hereby request the Board of Directors take the steps necessary to amend our bylaws and each appropriate governing document to give holders with an aggregate of 20% net long of our outstanding common stock the power to call a special shareowner meeting. This proposal does not impact our Board's current power to call a special meeting."

(c) The "Shareholders request that the Board of Directors prohibit sales of facial recognition technology to government agencies unless the Board concludes, after an evaluation using

(continued)

[67] https://www.sec.gov/Archives/edgar/data/1018724/000119312519102995/d667736ddef14a.htm, p. 15 ff.

independent evidence, that the technology does not cause or contribute to actual or potential violations of civil and human rights."

(d) The "Shareholders request the Board of Directors commission an independent study of Recognition and report to shareholders regarding: The extent to which such technology may endanger, threaten, or violate privacy and or civil rights, and unfairly or disproportionately target or survey people of colour, immigrants and activists in the United States; The extent to which such technologies may be marketed and sold to authoritarian or repressive foreign governments, identified by the United States Department of State Country Reports on Human Rights Practices; The financial or operational risks associated with these human rights issues."

(e) The "Investors request that Amazon report on its efforts to address hate speech and the sale of offensive products throughout its businesses. The report should be produced at reasonable cost, exclude proprietary information and discuss Amazon's process to develop policies to address hate speech and offensive products, the experts and stakeholders it consulted while developing these policies and the enforcement mechanisms it has put in place, or intends to put in place, to ensure compliance."

(f) The "Shareholders ask the Board of Directors to adopt a policy, and amend the bylaws as necessary, to require the Chair of the Board to be an independent director. The policy should provide that (i) if the Board determines that a Chair who was independent when selected is no longer independent, the Board shall select a new Chair who satisfies the policy within 60 days of that determination; and (ii) compliance with this policy is waived if no independent director is available and willing to serve as Chair."

(g) The "Shareholders request management review its policies related to sexual harassment to assess whether the Company needs to adopt and implement additional policies and to report its findings, omitting proprietary information and prepared at a reasonable expense by December 31, 2019."

(h) The "Shareholders request that Amazon's Board of Directors prepare a public report as soon as practicable describing how Amazon is planning for disruptions posed by climate change, and how Amazon is reducing its company-wide dependence on fossil fuels. The report should be prepared at reasonable expense and may exclude confidential information."

(i) The "Shareholders request the Board adopt a policy to disclose to shareholders the following: A description of the specific minimum qualifications that the Board's nominating committee believes must be met by a nominee to be on the board of directors; and Each nominee's skills, ideological perspectives, and experience presented in a chart or matrix form. The disclosure shall be presented to the shareholders through the annual proxy statement and the Company's website within six (6) months of the date of the annual meeting and updated on an annual basis."

(j) The "Shareholders request Amazon report on the company's global median gender pay gap, including associated policy, reputational, competitive, and operational risks, and risks related to recruiting and retaining female talent. The report should be prepared at reasonable cost, omitting proprietary information, litigation strategy and legal compliance information. The gender pay gap is defined as the difference between male and female median earnings expressed as a percentage of male earnings (Organization for Economic Cooperation and Development)."

(k) The "Shareholders request the Board Compensation Committee prepare a report assessing the feasibility of integrating sustainability metrics, including metrics regarding diversity among senior executives, into performance measures or vesting conditions that may apply to senior executives under the Company's compensation plans or arrangements. For the purposes of this proposal, "sustainability" is defined as how environmental and social considerations, and related financial impacts, are integrated into long-term corporate strategy, and "diversity" refers to gender, racial, and ethnic diversity."

(l) The "Shareholders ask the Board to take steps to amend Company governing documents to provide that all non-binding matters presented by shareholders shall be decided by a simple majority of the votes cast FOR and AGAINST an item. This policy would apply to all such matters unless shareholders have approved higher thresholds, or applicable laws or stock exchange regulations dictate otherwise." To explain this proposal is to clarify that Amazon (like many other companies) uses the so-called "formula swapping" and counts ABSTAIN votes into the formula against

(continued)

shareholder proposals; that is, it mathematically converts every abstention into an AGAINST vote, reducing the percentage of votes cast in favor.[68]

All the shareholders' proposals were rejected at the general meeting.

4.3.9.2 Voting Mechanisms at General Meetings and Proxies

Voting mechanisms at general meetings may vary depending on state legislation and on the certificate of incorporation or bylaws. In addition, they vary depending on whether the resolution refers to the election of directors or to other items on the agenda (even if all these items are voted upon during the same general meeting).

With reference to *directors' election*, shareholders can vote either FOR or WITHHOLD (i.e., voting AGAINST is not allowed). Moreover, there are two mechanisms generally used by listed corporations: plurality and majority.

The *plurality voting mechanism* means that a director may win if she/he acquires the most votes cast. But *withheld votes are not cast or counted.* Assume the quorum is 500; even if a director is voted *FOR* by 100 and 400 WITHOLD their votes, he/she wins. If the *majority voting mechanism* applies, a director wins if she/he acquires the majority of the quorum (250 + 1 out of 500).

With reference to nonlisted companies, there is a third possible voting mechanism—*cumulative* voting—that improves the likelihood of minority representation on the board. If this mechanism applies, each shareholder gets votes equal to the number of shares owned multiplied by the number of seats to be filled.

Example of the Cumulative Voting Mechanism

Corp. J has 300 shares and two shareholders; shareholder A owns 199 shares, and shareholder B owns 101 shares. Corp. J has a *three-person board* elected to annual terms. If the majority voting applies, A would win each seat 199–101. If the cumulative voting applies, B casts 303 shares *all for one* candidate (who will be guaranteed to get one seat on the board) because A's 597 votes cannot be divided three ways so that all three are greater than 303.

[68]With reference to the debate about the "race to the top or to the bottom" in the competition of states' legislation (see Section 4.3 above), this is another interesting example. As the board explains in the opposition to this proposal, the vote-counting methodology, called "formula swapping," is consistent with Delaware law, where Amazon is incorporated. Section 216 of the Delaware General Corporation Law provides, as a default rule, that "in all matters other than the election of directors, the affirmative vote of the majority of shares present in person or represented by proxy at the meeting and entitled to vote on the subject matter shall be the act of the shareholders. Because shares that vote to abstain are present and entitled to vote, under this Delaware law standard any shares present at the meeting that abstain from voting are essentially counted as votes against the matter." This is a typical provision that undermines shareholders' votes and for which it is hard to find any reasonable justification, especially if we consider that, under the same provision, a different methodology applies if the vote is on the election of directors: in that case, an abstain vote does not count as an against vote.

The most common voting mechanism among listed corporations was plurality; however, since 2010 or so, shareholders (in particular institutional investors) have been trying to induce corporations to change their bylaws (through shareholders' proposals under Rule 14a-8) from plurality to majority voting. Currently, over 70% of S&P 500 companies have majority voting.

Shareholders may vote in person or by a proxy, that is, by finding a representative (proxy) who goes to the meeting and votes on its behalf or by merely sending out a document (also called proxy) duly filled to express the vote.

4.3.9.3 Election of Directors by Shareholders in Listed Companies

To put it simply, it is very difficult for shareholders to actually elect directors despite the fact that at law they have the power to appoint them.[69] This is due to many reasons. First of all, the composition of American listed companies, usually dispersed (see para. 3.2 above), makes it very difficult for any shareholder to solicit proxies in favor of its own nominees as also directors are allowed to solicit proxies and have interest to send them out and request votes. Therefore, there might be *proxy fights* between the list of nominees filed by the incumbent directors, on one side, and that by the shareholders on the other side. In these proxy fights, directors have control over corporate information and corporation proxy materials, and there is no general right for shareholders to *access all information*. We find different approaches according to states. Under the Delaware approach, for books and records, the burden is on the shareholder to show a "proper purpose"; for a shareholder list, the burden is on the corporation to show an "improper purpose" (DGCL, Section 220(c)). It can be noted that the directors' discretion is high when it comes to evaluating whether proper or improper purpose occurs. The MBCA specifically enumerates documents (shareholder lists, excerpts from board minutes, shareholder meeting minutes, and accounting records) that can be accessed if a shareholder shows "proper purpose" (MBCA, Sections 16.02, 16.01(e)). Finally, the New York state has adopted a hybrid approach—a statutory right to inspect key financial statements, stock lists, and shareholder meeting minutes is provided if a proper purpose (Section 624(a)–(e)) is shown, and there is a "catch-all" provision under Section 624(f) for books and records, according to which "Nothing herein contained shall impair the power of courts to compel the production for examination of the books and records of a corporation."

In addition, solicitation occurs at the *corporate expense* when directors solicit proxies, while if proxies are solicited by shareholders, generally they shall pay such costs by themselves: to solicit proxies, a shareholder must mail to all other shareholders, at the shareholder's own expense, drafting an independent proxy solicitation statement that complies with the requirements under Section 14 of the Securities Exchange Act 1934. There are *reimbursement rules* for shareholders in certain cases, but they can differ on, at least, three dimensions: the amount (all, part, or nothing?), conditionality (do you need to win to be reimbursed?), and bias (favor

[69] The leading critique of the voting system comes from Bebchuk (2007), pp. 687–695.

incumbents, insurgents, or neither). The Delaware Supreme Court invited resolutions adopted under Rule14a-8 to require the reimbursement of shareholders' proxy expenses; however, not all companies have adopted reimbursement rules. It is true that under the e-proxy rules (i.e., 17 CFR, Section 240.14a–16), both incumbents and insurgents can file proxy materials on a website, substantially reducing proxy solicitation costs. However, expenses may also include advertisements in newspapers, paying external consultants/providers specialized in shareholder identification, solicitation strategies, engagement with shareholders, encouraging shareholders to submit proxy votes, etc.

Therefore, incumbent directors are better off compared to shareholders in proxy fights: usually, directors win as they have more information, more money, and more power. Basically, only big shareholders or hedge funds and institutional investors have enough resources to target CEOs and other directors and run a proxy fight to displace them, but this generally occurs in the case of hostile takeovers; otherwise, under a cost/benefit analysis, there is no convenience.[70] In addition, most public companies adopt the so-called "advance notice" in bylaws, which requires nominations to be received by the company several months before the general meeting.

One of the hottest topics in corporate governance is indeed *proxy access*, and many American companies fiercely oppose it: several times in the past, there were regulatory attempts to allow qualifying shareholders the ability to nominate directors and for those nominees to appear on the company's proxy statement. It might seem a trivial provision, but as was magnificently stated, "proxy access would have the profound effect of destigmatizing dissident slates. If major holders could nominate directors, and have them be viable candidates without a hostile campaign, this would bring a new level of accountability to management teams. Proxy access would practically institutionalize shareholder activism—you can see why companies are so afraid of it."[71]

It is worth presenting the latest attempt by the SEC to regulate proxy access. The Dodd-Frank Act, Section 971 (a)(b), in 2010, allowed the SEC to regulate the possibility for shareholders to use corporations' documents to solicit proxies for directors' elections. Consequently, *in August 2010, the SEC introduced Rule 14a-11* to the Code of Federal Regulations, according to which it was a mandatory rule for all US-listed companies allowing "shareholder or shareholder group that has owned 3% of the voting power (net) continuously for a 3-year period" to "nominate directors for up to 25% of the company's board seats at each election." The Rule required that the shareholder group must not have a purpose to gain control of the company and clarified that "if multiple qualified proposals" were presented, the "largest shareholder group gets to nominate."[72] In other words, Rule 14a-11

[70]Historically, among the most contentious proxy fights (both featuring staggered boards), the one by Karla Scherer vs R.P. Scherer and at BKF Capital are mentioned by Gramm (2016), pp. 122–130 and 170–175.

[71]Gramm (2016), p. 197.

[72]For a comment, see Verret (2011).

provided for no right of qualified shareholders to appoint directors but just for *their right to nominate candidates*, using the same proxy materials as the company, that is, adding these candidates to those filed by the board of directors; then it would have been left to the general meeting of shareholders the choice on which candidates to appoint through the voting mechanism (majority or plurality) adopted under the bylaws. But the Business Roundtable and the Chamber of Commerce (whose members are listed corporations and acting as "interested parties" under the Administrative Procedure Act), on September 29, 2010, started a legal suit against the SEC before the Court of Appeals for the District of Columbia Circuit, asking the Court "to hold the Commission's rules unlawful under the Investment Company Act, Securities Exchange Act, and Administrative Procedure Act, to vacate the rules and their requirements, to issue a permanent injunction prohibiting the Commission from implementing and enforcing the requirements, and for such other relief as the Court deems appropriate." The reasons were that "the Proxy Access Rules are arbitrary and capricious and otherwise not in accordance with law; do not promote efficiency, competition, and capital formation; exceed the Commission's authority; and violate issuers' rights under the First and Fifth Amendments to the United States Constitution. Petitioners have asked the Commission to stay the rules, including their November 15, 2010 effective date, pending the conclusion of this litigation." To understand the petition, it is worth explaining that the SEC has the power to issue rules pursuant to the grant of authority under statutes. But its authority is not unlimited as rules must be consistent with the intent of Congress. Parties that are adversely affected by an SEC rule can go to court to challenge the rule as improper. On October 4, 2010, the Court issued an order granting stay; the final decision was released on July 22, 2011—the *Business Roundtable et al. v. Securities and Exchange Commission* case.[73]

Business Roundtable et al. v. Securities and Exchange Commission

The Court summarized the reasons for introducing Rule 14 a-11, as explained by the SEC (who voted 3 vs. 2), that is, to create "potential benefits of improved board and company performance and shareholder value" sufficient to "justify [its] potential costs." Meanwhile, a private ordering and state law to facilitate shareholders "would not be as effective and efficient." Petitioners, on the other hand, argued that the SEC "acted arbitrarily and capriciously here because it neglected its statutory responsibility to determine the likely economic consequences of Rule 14a-11 and to connect those consequences to efficiency, competition, and capital formation." Under the Administrative Procedure Act, courts will set aside an agency action that is "arbitrary, capricious, an abuse of discretion, or otherwise not in accordance with law." Therefore, courts must assure that the agency has "examine[d] the relevant data and articulate[d] a satisfactory explanation for its action including a rational connection between the facts found and the choices made." The Commission also has a "statutory obligation to determine as best it can the *economic implications* of the rule." Indeed, the Commission has a unique obligation to consider the effect of a new rule upon "*efficiency*, competition, and capital formation." Its failure to "apprise itself—and hence the public and the Congress—of the economic consequences of a proposed regulation" makes the promulgation of the rule arbitrary and capricious and not in accordance with the law.
What did the Court believe? Did the SEC act arbitrarily and capriciously? According to the Court,

(continued)

[73] *Business Roundtable v. SEC* – 396 U.S. App. D.C. 259, 647 F.3d 1144 (2011).

the SEC failed to assess economic effects, was inconsistent in framing the costs and benefits of the rule, failed to quantify certain costs or to explain why those costs could not be quantified, neglected to support its predictive judgments, contradicted itself, and failed to respond to the substantial problems raised by the commenters. As benefits of the Rule, the SEC identified "direct cost savings" for shareholders, in part due to "reduced printing and postage costs" and reduced expenditures for advertising compared to those of a "traditional" proxy contest; "mitigation of the collective action and free-rider concerns"; and the "potential of creating the benefit of improved board performance and enhanced shareholder value." As for costs, the SEC identified "preparation of required disclosure, printing and mailing . . ., and additional solicitations" and "adverse effects on company and board performance" by distracting management. But the Court contested that the directors' expenditure in challenging the shareholders' nominee was not specified in the amount and was "mere speculation" by the SEC and also that for the improvement of board performance and increased shareholder value, empirical data were insufficient as there are contradictory studies in the literature in one sense and another. Despite these inaccuracies, the SEC nonetheless concluded that the rule would promote the "efficiency of the economy on the whole" and that the benefits of the rule would "justify the costs" of the rule. But it did not quantify the costs and benefits, did not consider the consequences of union and state pension funds using the rule, and did not evaluate the frequency with which shareholders would initiate election contests. For the foregoing reasons, the Court held that the Commission *was arbitrary and capricious* in promulgating Rule 14a-11; the petition was granted, and the *Rule was vacated.*

Later, upon initiative from institutional investors, under Rule 14a-8 of the Code of Federal Regulations, some companies have amended their bylaws in order to introduce provisions on proxy access by shareholders. However, the requirements for filing a list of candidates for election to the board of directors, to be included in a company's proxy materials, are very burdensome. For example, at Apple, one or more shareholders (but not more than 20) holding at least 3% of the share capital, and for at least 3 years, may file a list of nominees up to 20% of the members of the board of directors (e.g., in a board with eight members, 20% is equal to one member). But looking at the ownership pattern in US-listed companies, the biggest 20 pension funds do *not* reach 3% of the share capital in most companies. The conclusion is that for shareholders, it is almost impossible to file a list of nominees.

References

Barzuza M (2009) The State of State Antitakeover Law. Vand Law Rev 95:1973

Barzuza M (2024) Nevada v. Delaware: the New Market for Corporate Law. European Corporate Governance Institute – Law Working Paper No. 761/2024

Bebchuk LA (2007) The Myth of the Shareholder Franchise. Va Law Rev 93(3):675–732

Bebchuk LA, Tallarita R (2020) The Illusory Promise of Stakeholder Governance. Cornell Law Rev 106:91–177

Bebchuk LA, Cohen A, Spamann H (2010) The Wages of Failure: Executive Compensation at Bear Stearn and Lehman 2000-2008. Yale J Regul 27:257–282

Berglöf E (1997) A note on the typology of financial systems. In: Hopt KJ, Wymeersch E (eds) Comparative corporate governance. Essays and materials. De Gruyter, Berlin, p 151

Berle AA, Means G (1932) The modern corporation and private property. Transaction Publishers, New Brunswick, London

Brunetti A (1948) Trattato del diritto delle società. Giuffrè, Milano

Chandler AD Jr (1977) The visible hand: the managerial revolution in American business. Harvard University Press, Cambridge

Cooke CA (1950) Corporation, trust and company. An essay in legal history. Manchester University Press, Manchester

Davis JS (1917) Essays in the earlier history of American Corporations, vol I, II. Harvard University Press, Cambridge

Dubois AB (1938) The English business company after the Bubble Act 1720-1800. Octagon Books, New York

Dunlavy CA (2006) Social conceptions of the corporation: insights from the history of shareholder voting rights. Wash Lee Law Rev 63:1347–1388

Fama EF, Jensen MC (1983) Separation of ownership and control. J Law Econ 26(3):301–325

Franks J, Mayer C (1995) Ownership and control. In: Siebert H (ed) Trends in business or-ganization: do participation and cooperation increase competitiveness? Mohr JCB, Tübingen, p 171

Franks J, Mayer C (2017) Evolution of ownership and control around the world: the changing face of capitalism. Finance Working Paper N°503/2017, p 44

Friedman M (1970) The social responsibility of business is to increase its profits. New York Times, Sunday Magazine, Sept. 13, p 32

Galgano F (2007) La forza del numero e la legge della ragione. Storia del principio di maggio-ranza. Il Mulino, Bologna

Gevurtz FA (2004) Historical and political origins of the corporate board of directors. Hofstra Law Rev 33(1):89–173

Gramm J (2016) Dear Chairman. Boardroom Battles and the rise of shareholders activism. HarperCollins Publishers, New York

Greenspon J (2019) How big a problem is it that a few shareholders own stock in so many competing companies? Harv Bus Rev. at https://hbr.org/2019/02/how-big-a-problem-is-it-that-a-few-shareholders-own-stock-in-so-many-competing-companies

Hansmann H, Kraakman R, Squire R (2005-2006) Law and the rise of the firm. Harv Law Rev 119(5):1333–1403

Harris R (2005) The formation of East India Company as a Cooperation – Enhancing Institution, at SSRN: http://ssrn.com/abstract=874406

Hart O, Zingales L (2022) The new corporate governance. Univ Chic Bus Law Rev 1(1):195

Holdsworth WS (1926) A history of English law, vol IX. Sweet & Maxwell Ltd, London

Kraakman RH et al (2017) The anatomy of corporate law. A comparative and functional approach. Oxford University Press, Oxford

Lewellen J., Lewellen K (2022), The ownership of U.S. Corporations, at https://ssrn.com/abstract=4173466

Lipton M, Cain KL, Iannone KC (2019) Stakeholder governance and the fiduciary duties of directors. Harvard Law School Forum on Corporate Governance, https://corpgov.law.harvard.edu/2019/08/24/stakeholder-governance-and-the-fiduciary-duties-of-directors/

Macey JR (2020) The central role of myth in Corporate Law. In: ECGI working paper series in law, Working Paper N° 519/2020, p 25

Maitland FW (1911) The unincorporate body, Collected papers, vol III. Cambridge University Press, Cambridge

Mazzuccato M (2018) The value of everything. Making and taking in the global economy. Allen Lane, Great Britain

Morrissey DJ (2013) Executive compensation and income inequality. William Mary Bus Law Rev 4(1):1–35

O' Donnell C (1952) Origins of the corporate executive. Bull Bus Hist Soc 26(2):55–72

Pinto AR (2011) The United States. In: Bruno S, Ruggiero E (eds) Public companies and the role of shareholders, National models towards global integration. Wolters Kluwer, p 20

Roe MJ (1994) Strong managers weak owners, The political roots of American corporate finance. Princeton University Press, Princeton

Roe MJ (2003) Delaware's competition. Harv Law Rev 117:588–646
Romano R (1993) State competition for corporate charters. In: Romano R (ed) Foundations of corporate law. Oxford University Press, Oxford, p 87
Strine LE Jr (2015) The dangers of denial: The need for a clear-eyed understanding of the power and accountability structure established by the Delaware General Corporation Law. Wake For Law Rev 50:761
Strine LE, Jr, Hammermesh LA, Balotti RF, Gorris JM (2009) Loyalty's core demand: the defining role of good faith in corporation law. The Harvard John M. Olin Discussion Paper Series, Discussion Paper N. 630, p 3, N. 3/2009
The Committee on Corp. Laws of the Am. Bar Ass'n (1990) Other constituencies statutes: potential for confusion. Bus Lawyer 45(4):2253–2271
The Lawes or Standing Orders of the East India Company (1621), Allde E, London
Verret JW (2011) Defending against shareholder proxy access: Delaware's future reviewing company defenses in the era of Dodd–Frank. J Corp Law 36(2):393

Public Companies: UK Law

5

Contents

5.1 UK Companies: Sources of Law

The United Kingdom is a common law jurisdiction. However, the main source of company law is the *Companies Act (CA) dated 2006*, which has been in force since November 2008.[1] Many of the provisions contained in the Act have been inserted, over the years, to implement European directives and are therefore common to other European jurisdictions: the United Kingdom was part of the European Union until 31 January 2020, when the so-called "Brexit" took place based on a referendum held on 23 June 2016. The provisions deriving from European directives are still in force despite the UK's exit from the European Union (see Sections 6.1 and 6.2 below on European directives). The Companies Act is completed by the *Model Articles of*

[1]The Companies Act 2006, https://www.legislation.gov.uk/ukpga/2006/46/contents.

[2]See at https://www.handbook.fca.org.uk/handbook/LR.pdf.

S. Bruno, *Foundations of Business and Company Law*,
https://doi.org/10.1007/978-3-031-71885-4_5

Association, drafted by the Secretary of State, which function as standard default articles that a company can use; by way of regulation, the Model Articles are provided as a schedule to the Companies Act 2006. There are three different Model Articles for each type of company. Under the Companies Act 2006, the *types of companies* are private companies limited by shares, private companies limited by guarantee, and public companies.

The articles of association adopted by companies are an additional source of law. Moreover, the United Kingdom being a common law jurisdiction, also case law is a source of law therein.

For listed companies, an additional source of law is the UK Listing Authority Rules, issued by the Financial Conduct Authority (*Listing Rules*).[2]

Finally, the *Corporate Governance Code* has to be mentioned, even if it is a source of *soft law*, that is, a set of principles addressing listed companies that are not binding. The United Kingdom has been the first jurisdiction worldwide to have adopted a code of best practice, the Cadbury Code, issued in 1992, to promote best practices with reference only to listed companies. It defined corporate governance as "the system by which companies are directed and controlled." When the modern corporate governance debate emerged in the early 1990s, the government preferred to leave the issue to a business initiative, with governmental support, rather than directly regulating it.[3] Other codes followed, such as the Greenbury Code on directors' remuneration in 1995 and the Hampel Code on corporate governance in 1998. The original Cadbury Code has been revised many times since 1992. In particular, it was revised further to various reports released in 2003 (and highlighting some malfunctioning in UK companies), namely, the Higgs Report on nonexecutive directors (NEDs), the Smith Report on audit committees, the Report of the Co-ordinating group on audit and accounting issues, and the Review of the regulatory regime of the accountancy profession. Eventually, the separate codes were combined in the *UK Corporate Governance Code*, the latest edition of which was published in January 2024; it was issued by the Financial Reporting Council.[4] As explained the Code is not a set of rules but of recommendations and therefore it is not binding. However, all companies with listed equity shares in UK are required to report in annual report and accounts on how they have applied the Code's principles and either to confirm compliance or explaining why they have not, the so called *comply-or-explain rule*" stated under the Listing Rules. The rationale is that through disclosure, compliance is fostered: for companies who do not comply reputational adverse effects on investment decision in the market is the (assumed) sanction. We can say that the level of compliance with the Code is indeed high. The UK Corporate Governance Code is made of five sections dealing with:

1. Board leadership and company purpose
2. Division of responsibilities

[3]Davies (2002), pp. 200–202.

[4]See https://media.frc.org.uk/documents/UK_Corporate_Governance_Code_2024_kRCm5ss.pdf.

3. Composition, succession, and evaluation
4. Audit, risk, and internal control
5. Remuneration

Each section is made of principles and provisions. The Listing Rules require companies to make a statement on how they have applied the principles in the context of the particular circumstances of the company, including how the board has set the company's purpose and strategy, met objectives, and achieved outcomes through the decisions it has taken, and also require companies to set out their reasons for noncompliance with the provisions. Companies may depart from the Code for a number of reasons, e.g., size, ownership structure, history, etc.[5] The Code is also supported by the UK Corporate Governance Guidance, meant to stimulate thinking on how boards can carry out their role most effectively.[6]

5.2 Ownership Pattern in the UK

As above mentioned (see Section 4.2 above), the UK can also be qualified as an outside financial system characterized by very few blockholders and widely dispersed shares, though not as much as in the US financial market. Looking at the average ownership structure of listed companies at the end of 2022, we can note that:

- Pension funds and insurance companies owned 2.4%.
- Banks held 3.4%.
- Unit trusts held 0.5%.
- Investment trusts owned 0.7%.
- Other financial institutions held 12.2%.
- Overseas investors owned 17.1%.
- Individuals owned 3.9%.
- The public sector held 0.5%.
- Multiple ownership pooled nominees held 50.6%.
- Charities held 0.2%.
- Private nonfinancial companies owned 1.5%.
- Excluded held 7%.[7]

As can be seen, the majority of shares, based on average, belong to the institutional investors, including overseas investors (i.e., pension funds, insurance

[5] ID, p 4.

[6] Ibidem.

[7] See Office for National Statics, at https://www.ons.gov.uk/economy/investmentspensionsandtrusts/datasets/ownershipofukshares.

[8] Mazzuccato (2018), p. 144.

[9] See OECD, Corporate Governance Factbook 2021 (2021), https://www.oecd.org/corporate/OECD-Corporate-Governance-Factbook.pdf, p. 13; Sergakis (2023), p. 2.

companies, banks, unit and investment trusts, other financial institutions, and multiple ownership pooled nominees; prevalence and strength are for pension funds).

In the United States and in the United Kingdom, there had been a transformation over the years in the ownership pattern: in 1963, UK individuals used to own more than 50% of the stock market, while institutional investors accounted for about 10%; since then, the trend has been completely reversed.[8] The reconcentration of ownership within institutional investment schemes (mostly but not solely in the United Kingdom and the United States) has been a more recent characteristic of financial markets, with institutional investors holding, on average, 43% of the listed companies' share capital at the global scale.[9]

For example, Burberry Group Plc capital is composed of 0.07% individual insiders, 0.1% private companies, 0.2% state or government, 0.6% employee share scheme, and 2.9% general public, and the remaining 96.13% are held by institutional investors (at the top of which are Schroder Investment Management Ltd. with 10.38%, Blackrock Inc. with 8.99%, Vanguard with 4.43%, etc.).[10]

At Shell, institutional investors hold 65.6% (the top of which are Blackrock with 8.62%, Vanguard with 4.64%, Norges Bank Investment Management with 3.28%, State Street 1.75%, and UBS Asset Management AG with 1.49%), while individual insiders hold 0.2%, the state or government 0.1%, employee share scheme 0.4%, private companies 1.8%, and the general public 32.0%.[11]

5.3 How to Set Up a Corporation: Types of Corporations

Companies are registered with the Registrar of Companies according to the Companies Act 2006. An electronic facility for registering companies online is provided. The registration process is very simple; there is ease of access to the corporate form. Neither formalities nor barriers of any substance are placed in the way of obtaining a corporate status. The methods for forming a company are provided under Sections 7–13 CA 2006 and are summarized below.

Two documents are required by the Companies Act to be registered: memorandum of association and articles of association.

In the *memorandum of association* (or *memorandum*), the names of the founding members are included. It serves as evidence of the intention of subscribers to form a company and become members of the company in formation. So it will not be possible to amend or update the memorandum in the future since its purpose is very limited in scope.

The *articles of association* (or the *company's constitution*) are rules that govern the conduct of internal affairs. The internal allocation of powers between the directors and the members of the company is set out in the articles of association.

[10] https://simplywall.st/stocks/gb/consumer-durables/lse-brby/burberry-group-shares/ownership.

[11] https://simplywall.st/stocks/gb/energy/lse-shel/shell-shares/ownership.

They form, at law, a *statutory contract* between the company and its members and among its members.

As mentioned, the types of companies are:

1. *Private company*: it is defined as "a company which is not public" (Section 4 CA 2006). It may be set up even with only one member. There is no capital requirement. Capital can be divided into shares or quotas. However, the shares, quotas, or debentures *shall not be offered to the public*: they may be issued but placed in private investors. By private investors mean those who already have a relationship with the company, e.g., employees (including their relatives), debenture holders, and creditors. In the case of offers to the public, the Secretary of State has the power to sanction a private company by ordering its reregistration as a public company, but the offer to the public is valid. This is the most important model in the UK, considering the number of private companies, which reaches around 99% of all the registered companies. Private companies have tax advantages compared to public companies; additionally, the model is used by small and medium-sized enterprises, which actually are the dominant business models in the UK. Private companies usually have a few members. The Companies Act 2006 provides for private companies limited by shares (the most common type), private companies limited by guarantee (with a share capital or without a share capital), and unlimited companies (there is no limited liability for members).
2. *Public company*: it may offer shares and other financial instruments to the public. The authorized minimum share capital is 50,000 sterling, and all the rules to maintain the integrity of the capital, introduced by the II EU Directive (see Section 6.2 below), apply. It may be set up even with one member. It is the most important model for companies in terms of capitalization. Only public companies may be listed on regulated markets.

5.4 Allocation of Powers Between the General Meeting of Shareholders and the Board of Directors

The Companies Act 2006 establishes the powers allocated to the general meeting of shareholders. They are:

1. Appointment and removal of directors
2. Appointment, removal, and fixing the remuneration of external auditors (accounting control from external auditors is required for all companies)
3. Approval of identified transactions where directors' conflict of interests may arise (such as directors' long-term service contracts; the sale of substantial property transactions where the counterparty is one or more directors; loans, quasi-loans, and credit transactions to directors; payment for loss of office)
4. Amendment to the company's constitution (i.e., articles of association)
5. Approval of share buybacks and redemption of redeemable shares

In all such cases, the authority of the general meeting is *mandatory*. Any transaction in breach of the provision would be declared null and void, and the directors would be liable for damages to the company as a consequence thereof. In addition, the company's constitution could not provide anything different from the powers allocated by CA 2006 to the general meeting of shareholders.

As for the *removal* of directors, in particular, Section 168 CA 2006 states:

> (1) A company may by ordinary resolution at a meeting remove a director before the expiration of his period of office, notwithstanding anything in any agreement between it and him.

The removal can be voted *at will*, which means with or without cause; as said, also this power is *mandatory* and could never be limited or excluded by the company's constitution.

In addition to the powers above mentioned, for *listed companies*, the general meeting shall have the power to approve:

1. The directors' remuneration report for the following financial year: the general meeting vote has, since October 2013, been *binding* and must therefore be followed by the board of directors.
2. Political donations, defined as "donations made by companies to political parties, to other political organizations and to independent election candidates, and political expenditure incurred by companies" (see Sections 362–378 CA 2006 for more detail)—without the general meeting approval, directors are directly liable to reimburse the company for any damage or loss incurred.
3. In case of takeovers, any defensive measure to contrast the takeover and to subsequently modify the resolutions previously adopted.
4. Larger transactions (under the Listing Rules, N. 10.2), i.e., those substantial transactions that are out of the ordinary course of the company's business—the criteria are specified to identify and classify those transactions, depending upon their incidence on the company's assets (in terms of profit, consideration of the nature of transaction, etc.). If this percentage ratio is 25% or more, directors must obtain the general meeting approval before entering into that transaction. Any agreement affecting the transaction is conditional upon the obtainment of such approval (see the Listing Rules, N. 10.5.1).

As for the power to manage the company, it is typically allocated to the *board of directors*, even though there is no such provision in the Companies Act 2006. It is the Model Articles of Association (Section 3) that, for all types of companies, provide:

[12] See https://www.gov.uk/government/publications/model-articles-for-private-companies-limited-by-shares/model-articles-for-private-companies-limited-by-shares.

> Subject to the Articles, the directors are responsible for the management of the company's business, for which purpose they may exercise all the powers of the company.[12]

However, as above explained, the Model Articles are a set of default rules that can be freely amended by each company. Therefore, this is not a mandatory rule; the consequence is that, in theory, each company could allocate one or more managerial powers to the general meeting of shareholders, even though, in practice, management is generally allocated to the directors. In addition, it is interesting to consider that the same Model Articles (Section 4) provide a "members' reserve power," according to which (for all types of companies):

> (1) The members may, by special resolution, direct the directors to take, or refrain from taking, specified action; (2) No such special resolution invalidates anything which the directors have done before the passing of the resolution. In other words, if anything different is not provided by a company, shareholders have always the power to guide directors on how to manage the company and also to bar any action on which shareholders do not agree; they should vote by special resolution in a shareholders' meeting.

This interesting provision can be said to be the descendant of the original conception of the general meeting of shareholders under the first model of the British company, with a clear hierarchy between shareholders and directors in favor of the former (see Section 4.1 above). In any case, from the analysis of all the provisions above presented, it is evident that the relationship between the general meeting of shareholders and the board of directors is reversed when compared with US public companies: first of all, under UK company law, the shareholders have much more powers than under US law; second, it can be inferred that primacy in governing the company is located on shareholders over directors. Directors are fiduciaries to the shareholders, and they can be removed upon the latter's will. While the shareholders' powers are mandatorily fixed by the Companies Act, managerial powers do not exclusively belong to the directors as each company may decide, at least in theory, where to allocate managerial powers and define them.[13]

5.5 The Functioning of the General Meeting of Shareholders

The general meeting of shareholders may adopt *ordinary* or *special resolutions* (Sections 281 ff. CA 2006): the first type is approved by a simple majority of shareholders, while the latter is approved by a 75% majority and is generally required by law for most important decisions.

[13]To expand on the comparison between English and American laws, also with reference to the historical foundations of the relationship between shareholders and directors, see Bruno (2012).

The power to call a general meeting is allocated, under Sections 302 ff CA 2006, to the board of directors. In addition, shareholders reaching a 5% threshold or at least 100 of them representing an average of at least GBP£100 each (GBP£10,000 collectively) may require the board of directors to move a resolution for the general meeting (Section 338 CA 2006). Moreover, for listed companies, shareholders reaching 2.5% have the power to ask the board to add one or more items to the agenda of the general meeting. Any request by the shareholders to circulate a resolution or to add an item to the agenda is valid, and the board must table the resolution or the item to the agenda unless the board shows that the request is ineffective (because it is inconsistent with any enactment or with the company's constitution or otherwise), defamatory to any person, frivolous, or vexatious. In other words, apart from the latter exceptions, shareholders reaching the mentioned thresholds have a *right* to file a resolution or to add one or more items to the agenda. These provisions, with reference to listed corporations, have been introduced in the Companies Act to implement European Directive N. 2007/36/EC on *shareholders' rights*, aiming to foster the *voice* of the shareholders in general meetings of listed companies, as will be analyzed by Section 6.2 below.

In addition, it is worth mentioning also Section 1, Provision n. 4), of the UK Corporate Governance Code, according to which:

> When 20% per cent or more of votes have been cast against the board recommendation for a resolution, the company should explain, when announcing voting results, what actions it intends to take to consult shareholders in order to understand the reasons behind the result. An update on the views received from shareholders and actions taken should be published no later than six months after the shareholder meeting. The board should then provide a final summary in the annual report and, if applicable, in the explanatory notes to resolutions at the next shareholder meeting, on what impact the feedback has had on the decisions the board has taken and any actions or resolutions now proposed.

This provision shows how the board of directors is encouraged to understand the views of the shareholders and take into due consideration any significant votes cast against a proposal by the board. Under the same section of the UK Corporate Governance Code, Provision n. 3), additionally, the chair of the board of directors is recommended to seek "regular engagement with major shareholders in order to understand their views on governance and performance against the strategy" and "should ensure that the board has a clear understanding of the views of shareholders," while the chairs of the Internal Committees (see below, Section 5.6.1) "should seek engagement with shareholders on significant matters related to their areas of responsibility." This approach, consisting in recommending directors to pursue a constant dialogue with shareholders and even understand their different views on issues, is a very important element for a clear comprehension on how UK-listed companies operate—an approach that is completely different from the US attitude.

However, as a matter of fact, the agenda for the meetings is usually determined by the board; counterproposals from the shareholders will often not be forthcoming, even though, in listed companies, institutional investors have recently been very active and bringing various items to the attention of the general meeting for votes. Shareholders' proposals may relate to the displacement of one or more directors; governance; social or environmental issues; health issues, or business proposals. Usually, general meetings confirm board proposals as majority shareholders normally cast their votes in favor of the board's recommendations.

In any case, the annual general meeting is seen as having a disciplinary effect: it is an event in which the board has to account to the market, and the English financial press is very inquisitive of it.

Shareholders may vote in person or through proxies, which can also be conferred on the members of the board of directors.

5.6 The Model of the Board of Directors and Delegation of Powers

The board model for all UK companies is the one-tier model, with the general meeting of shareholders and the board of directors.

Directors are generally appointed by the general meeting of shareholders, but this power is not mandatory under the Companies Act. They could, alternatively, be appointed by a decision of the other directors (see Model Articles of Association, Section 20). Also in this case, however, the general meeting has the power to remove directors at will (with or without cause). This power is mandatory under CA 2006: it cannot be limited or excluded by the articles, even though a director is appointed by other directors. In listed companies, the appointment of directors is done on an annual basis, but they can be reelected.

The Companies Act does not provide for any delegation of directors' powers nor for the internal organization of the board. It is the Model Articles of Association, Section 5, that states:

> Subject to the Articles, the directors may delegate any of the powers which are conferred on them under the articles — (a) to such person or committee . . .as they think fit.

On the other hand, Section 6 therein states:

> Committees to which the directors delegate any of their powers must follow procedures which are based as far as they are applicable on those provisions of the articles which govern the taking of decisions by directors. (2) The directors may make rules of procedure for all or any committees, which prevail over rules derived from the articles if they are not consistent with them.

In other words, the internal organization of the board and the setting up of internal committees and their powers, functions, and procedures are left to the shareholders' decision, as expressed in the company's articles of association or, alternatively, to the board itself. The autonomy and discretion of the shareholders or directors are therefore paramount, and there are no binding rules in this respect.

If director powers are delegated to one of them, these directors are called *executive directors*, while those directors who do not have any delegated power, that is, no managerial position in the company, and are just members of the board are called *nonexecutive directors*. This distinction was born in practice, and there is no reference to it whatsoever either in the Companies Act or in the Model Articles of Association. Despite the distinction, it is worth pointing out that boards are *collectively and unitarily conceived*; no dichotomy can be inferred between the executive and the nonexecutive directors. No provision of law contemplates specific internal supervision or control function over executive directors or managers by nonexecutive directors.

The board of directors appoints the chair, whose functions are not regulated by the Companies Act. It is the Corporate Governance Code that describes her/his responsibilities, which states under Section 2, Principle F, that:

> The chair leads the board and is responsible for its overall effectiveness in directing the company. They should demonstrate objective judgement throughout their tenure and promote a culture of openness and debate. In addition, the chair facilitates constructive board relations and the effective contribution of all non-executive directors, and ensures that directors receive accurate, timely and clear information.

The Corporate Governance Code also states that the chair should be independent and that the roles of the chair and the chief executive should not be exercised by the same individual (Section 2, Provision n. 9).

5.6.1 Nonexecutive Independent Directors

It is the Corporate Governance Code that contains some principles addressing nonexecutive directors. Indeed, it was particularly after the Higgs Report, mentioned above and published in 2003, that the Code was significantly amended to take into account the main findings of the Report.[14] The Report was, at the end, very diplomatic: its main conclusion was that the UK model is successful as no big scandals have occurred.[15] However, some critique on nonexecutive directors (NEDs) emerged from empirical research, which can be summarized as follows: (1) NEDs and executives belong to the same oligarchy; (2) NEDs are usually friends

[14] Higgs (2003).

[15] To expand on the topic, see Bruno (2004) pp. 897, 905–910.

of the executives: there is no public or objective selection for them as they are mostly chosen because of friendship (with low percentage of exceptions); (3) they do not show competence in business or finance; (4) they do not devote much time to the service (very few meetings are held in a year; on average, 15/30 days in a year are devoted to the company); and (5) shareholders do not want to meet them as they are not supposed to know much about the conduct of business. However, the situation has highly changed since then, also because subsequent Corporate Governance Codes have provided for more stringent recommendations addressing NEDs.

Under Section 2 of the Code on *Division of Responsibilities*, Principle G, it is stated:

> The board should include an appropriate combination of executive and non-executive (and, in particular, independent non-executive) directors, such that no one individual or small group of individuals dominates the board's decision making. There should be a clear division of responsibilities between the leadership of the board and the executive leadership of the company's business.

On the other hand, Principle H states:

> Non-executive directors should have sufficient time to meet their board responsibilities. They should provide *constructive challenge*, strategic guidance, offer specialist advice and hold management to account.

These two principles highlight the importance of NEDs, who should be appointed by an *appropriate number*; it is also recommended that they should have *sufficient time* to devote to the exercise of their function. More importantly, it is explained what their *role* is: challenging decisions, offering strategic guidance and specialist advice, as well as holding the management to account.

In addition, Provision n. 13) of the same section, elaborating more on their role, states:

> Non-executive directors have a prime role in appointing and removing executive directors. Non-executive directors should scrutinize and hold to account the performance of management and individual executive directors against agreed performance objectives. The chair should hold meetings with the non-executive directors without the executive directors present.

As for the selection of all directors (including NEDs), Section 3, on *Composition, Succession and Evaluation*, of the Corporate Governance Code, Principle J, explains:

> Appointments to the board should be subject to a formal, rigorous and transparent procedure, and an effective succession plan for the board and senior management should be maintained. Both appointments and succession plans should be based

> on merit and objective criteria. They should promote diversity, inclusion and equal opportunity.

With reference to selection, Provision n. 20 states:

> Open advertising and/or an external search consultancy should generally be used for the appointment of the chair and non-executive directors. If an external search consultancy is engaged it should be identified in the annual report alongside a statement about any other connection it has with the company or individual directors.

On diversity, Principle K states:

> The board and its committees should have a combination of skills, experience and knowledge. Consideration should be given to the length of service of the board as a whole and membership regularly refreshed.

Meanwhile, Principle L recommends:

> Annual evaluation of the board should consider its performance, composition, diversity and how effectively members work together to achieve objectives. Individual evaluation should demonstrate whether each director continues to contribute effectively.

In addition, it is important to highlight that, as mentioned, Principle G of the same Section 2 recommends the appointment of nonexecutive and *independent* directors, while Provision n. 11) states:

> At least half the board, excluding the chair, should be non-executive directors whom the board considers to be *independent*.

What is the meaning of independence, and what is the function of nonexecutive directors for the good functioning of corporate governance? It is Section 2, Provision 10, that offers a definition for independence. It is upon the board to identify annually those members who are deemed to be independent. In other words, the Code gives examples of situations that "are likely to impair, or could appear to impair" independence. This means, on one side, that there might also be other circumstances that may impair independence and, on the other side, that despite these situations, the board can assess whether independence occurs, providing a clear explanation. In any case, the final evaluation is always left to the board.

The situations are if a person:

1. Is or has been an employee of the company or group within the last 5 years
2. Has, or has had within the last 3 years, a material business relationship with the company, either directly or as a partner, shareholder, director, or senior employee of a body that has such a relationship with the company
3. Has received or receives additional remuneration from the company apart from a director's
4. Has close family ties with any of the company's advisers, directors, or senior employees
5. Holds cross-directorships or has significant links with other directors through involvement
6. Is another company or body
7. Represents a significant shareholder, or
8. Has served on the board for more than 9 years from the date of their first appointment

The Code does not define when a business relationship is "material" or when a shareholder is "significant": therefore, the discretion to assess independence is left to the board.

With reference to the role of independent directors, their main task is to be members of the internal committees, which may be set up, within the board, to better organize the fulfillment of directors' function, also with reference to topics on which conflicts of interests concerning executive directors may arise (namely, nomination or remuneration). The Corporate Governance Code provides for three internal committees meant to support the decision-making process of the board:

1. The *Nomination Committee*: the *majority* of its members should be independent nonexecutive directors. It leads the process for appointments, ensures that plans are in place for orderly succession to both board and senior management positions, and oversees the development of a diverse pipeline for succession. It proposes new directors to the board, which will then pass the proposal to the general meeting of shareholders. See Section 2, Provision n. 17).
2. The *Remuneration Committee*: its members are *all* independent nonexecutive directors. It determines the policy for the remuneration of executive directors and sets the remuneration for the chair, executive directors, and senior management. It also reviews the remuneration of the workforce and related policies and the alignment of incentives and rewards with the company's culture and takes all these into account when setting the policy for the remuneration of executive directors. Remuneration policies and practices should be designed to support strategies and promote long-term sustainable success and should be aligned to company purposes and values and be clearly linked to the successful delivery of the company's long-term strategy. Meanwhile, the remuneration of NEDs is decided in accordance with the articles of association or by the board, i.e., not decided by the remuneration committee, and their remuneration should not include share options or other performance-related elements. See Section 5, Principle P, and Provisions nn. 33), 34), 36).

3. The *Audit Committee*: the members of this committee are *all* independent nonexecutive directors. The main roles of the committee have been specified and expanded by the latest revision, in 2024, of the Corporate Governance Code, which has been amended, in particular, to address internal control by increasing its effectiveness. The main roles and responsibilities of the audit committee include monitoring the integrity of the financial statements of the company and any formal announcements relating to the company's financial performance and reviewing significant financial reporting judgments contained in them; providing advice (where requested by the board) on whether the annual report and accounts, taken as a whole, are fair, balanced, and understandable; providing information necessary for shareholders to assess the company's position and performance, business model, and strategy; complying with the "Audit Committees and the External Audit: Minimum Standard," which has been published by the Financial Reporting Council;[16] reviewing the company's risk management and internal control framework, unless expressly addressed by a separate board risk committee, composed of independent nonexecutive directors, or by the board itself; monitoring and reviewing the effectiveness of the company's internal audit function or, where there is none, considering annually whether there is a need for one and making a recommendation to the board; and reporting to the board how it has discharged its responsibilities. See Section 4, Provision n. 25).

Absent specific mandatory rules in legislation on NEDs' duties and roles, one might wonder what incentives they have in holding this position despite being merely modestly remunerated (especially when compared with executive directors). The answer is that they are motivated by reputational incentives to do a good job of overseeing executive directors and to enjoy public esteem of being so regarded.[17] From a theoretical viewpoint, the appointment of NEDs is part of the so-called trusteeship strategy that seeks to remove conflicts of interest *ex ante* to ensure that an agent (in this case, executive directors) will not obtain personal gains when running the company.[18]

5.6.2 Directors' Qualification

UK legislation does not provide for any qualification requirements to be appointed as a director in a company.

The Listing Rules, N. 14, Annex 1, however, provides for disclosure obligation on directors' diversity by presenting a format that must be set out whereby information on gender and ethnicity shall be published also specifying percentages and

[16] See at https://media.frc.org.uk/documents/Audit_Committees_and_the_External_Audit_Minimum_Standard.pdf.

[17] Davies (2002), pp. 99–101.

[18] Ibidem.

positions within the board. These are mere disclosure requirements as no diversity rule is mandatorily provided.

The Corporate Governance Code, Section 3, Principle J, as already mentioned, recommends that appointments be subject to a formal, rigorous, and transparent procedure, and an effective succession plan for the board and senior management should be set up, while Principle K of the same Code recommends that the board and its committees should have a combination of skills, experience, and knowledge. But as already explained, these are just recommendations.

5.7 Directors' Duties: The Success of the Company

The regulation of directors' duties and liabilities is addressed by the Companies Act 2006 and case law.

Section 170 CA specifies the scope and nature of the general duties of directors in Chapter 2, stating that those duties "are owed by a directors of a company to the company" itself. This means that only the company may enforce any breach of these duties.

The first general duty is that directors "must act in accordance with the company's constitution and only exercise powers for the purposes for which they are conferred" (*Section 171 CA*).

More specifically, *Section 172 CA* states that directors have the duty "to promote the success of the company."

What is meant by "success of the company?" The same section explains this notion by providing that a director shall act in a way that she/he considers, in good faith, to be most likely to promote the success of the company for the *benefit of its members as a whole* while having regard for the following factors listed in Section 172:

1. likely consequences of the decisions in the long term;
2. need to foster company's relationships with suppliers, customers and others;
3. interests of the company's employees;
4. impact of the company's operations on the community and the environment;
5. desirability for the company's to maintain a reputation for high standards of business conduct;
6. the need to act fairly as between the members of the company.

The list, however, is not exhaustive, as specified by the same section: it highlights areas of particular importance that reflect wider expectations of responsible business behavior. The decision as to what will promote the success of the company and what

[19] Giddens (1998), pp. 65–70; Blair (1998).

[20] For a critique of the nexus of contracts approach within the UK debate, see Dean (2001), pp. 5–10, 36–40; Wheeler (2002), pp. 14–20, 53–60.

constitutes such success is one to be taken following the director's *good faith judgment*.

This section has been very important as it has no precursor in common law. It should be highlighted that it was introduced in 2006, when the consideration of such values (the environment, for example) by the public opinion or the market, values which are now part of the sustainability or ESG (environmental, social, and governance) discourse, was not so common for business or in the general company law debate; in fact, no legislation in the world had similar provisions (and even nowadays, no other legislation is so explicit). Introduced in the wake of the general political Third Way theories,[19] Section 172 was meant to show a different model of capitalism and of public companies, overriding the nexus of the contract approach and aiming at recognizing corporate social responsibility by involving the consideration of various stakeholders' interests and needs within the public company.[20] The result has been a compromise, the so-called *enlightened shareholder value*, codified by Section 172, to be distinguished from "pure shareholder value" on one side and "stakeholderism" or "pluralist approach" on the other side. In particular, the enlightened shareholder value was preferred over the alternatively proposed "pluralist approach," which would have implied the duty for directors to balance different and conflicting interests, resulting in wider discretion and specular narrower liabilities;[21] if a stakeholderism approach is adopted by a legal system, stakeholders have the legitimacy to start a legal suit against the directors; finally, according to stakeholderism, the purpose in managing a company is to enhance stakeholders' benefits regardless of shareholder value.[22] On the other side, pure shareholder value means that in managing a company, directors shall only consider shareholders' interests (namely, the maximization of profits). The enlightened shareholder approach clearly highlights that the primary interest to be pursued by the directors is the success of the company "for the benefit of its members as a whole"; in so doing, directors are required to have regard to the listed factors, which, however, are not exhaustive since additional matters may be taken into consideration. So it would be erroneous to argue that the Companies Act 2006 has introduced a stakeholding public company model in the UK because the enumerated factors are merely instrumental to the main purpose to be pursued by the directors, which is the duty of ensuring the success of the company for the "benefit of its members as a whole": it is submitted that any regard for the factors listed in Section 172 (1) must be such that "it does not impinge on the members' benefits."[23] Section 170 of the Companies Act 2006 is the provision that introduces to all the duties contained in Part 10 of the Act:

---

[21] With reference to the "pluralist approach": Kelly and Parkinson (1998), p. 174; Roach (2001). For a comparison of the two models, see also Parkinson (2002), pp. 43–50.

[22] The literature on this topic is countless. However, a good explanation of the terminology can be found in Bebchuk and Tallarita (2020), pp. 108–115.

[23] Keay (2010), p. 31.

[24] Lowry (2009), pp. 607, 612.

[25] To expand on the topic, see also Bruno (2017), pp. 315–320.

it is the key "scoping" provision laying down that the general duties therein provided are owed by a director to the company itself and, consequentially, stakeholders, even if addressed by Section 172, have no legitimacy to enforce breach of those duties; only the company may enforce any breach of them.[24] Therefore, primacy is for shareholders, but directors shall take into consideration, instrumentally, also other stakeholders in order to pursue shareholder value. A few provisions have been more debated than Section 172.[25] However, consideration of the success of the company has also been confirmed under the latest edition of the Corporate Governance Code, whose Section 1, Principle A, states:

> A successful company is led by an effective and entrepreneurial board, whose role is to promote the long-term sustainable success of the company, generating value for shareholders and contributing to wider society. The board should ensure that the necessary resources, policies and practices are in place for the company to meet its objectives and measure performance against them.

In addition, in order to make the provisions under Section 172 CA more effective, the same Corporate Governance Code, Section 1, Provision n. 5, states:

> The board should understand the views of the company's other key stakeholders and describe in the annual report how these and the matters set out in section 172 of the Companies Act 2006 have been considered in board discussions and decision-making. The board should keep engagement mechanisms under review so that they remain effective.

That is, the Corporate Governance Code tries to ensure that Section 172 CA is actually applied by recommending the disclosure, in the annual report, of how stakeholders have been taken into consideration in board meetings and decision-making processes. In this respect, a particular regard is devoted to the workforce, among the stakeholders, for whom the same Provision n. 5) of the Corporate Governance Code states:

> For engagement with the workforce, one or a combination of the following methods should be used: a director appointed from the workforce; a formal workforce advisory panel; or a designated non-executive director. If the board has not chosen one or more of these methods, it should explain what alternative arrangements are in place and why it considers that they are effective.

These three alternatives are recommended to listed companies so they can engage with the workforce and be able to take due consideration of their interests.

With reference to the other provisions on directors' duties contained in the Companies Act, it has to be mentioned *Section 173 CA*, under which directors are required to exercise independent judgment while managing the company, which means that they shall not be driven by any personal interest that might influence their decision.

Moreover, *Section 174 CA* states that directors have the duty to exercise reasonable care, skill, and diligence. Judges shall apply subjective and objective tests to evaluate directors' conduct. Therefore directors shall exercise the same standard of care, skill, and diligence that would be exercised by a reasonably diligent person with:

(a) the general knowledge, skill and experience that may reasonably be expected of a person carrying out the same functions as the director in relation to that company (*objective test*); and,
(b) the general knowledge, skill and experience that the director actually has (*subjective test*).

In analyzing the duty of care, skill, and diligence of directors, may judges distinguish between executive and nonexecutive? No distinction can be drawn from the Companies Act. Both owe the same legal duties to the company. However, the time devoted is far less for nonexecutive directors than for executive directors; in addition, the former do not share the same detailed knowledge and experience in the company's affairs as executive directors. These matters may be relevant in assessing the knowledge, skill, and experience to be reasonably expected of a nonexecutive compared to what is to be reasonably expected from an executive (the "objective test"); therefore, from executive directors, higher knowledge, skill, and experience can be reasonably expected. However, in both cases, they have the duty to gather all available information and to be competent: a nonexecutive director cannot argue that she/he is not competent because if this is the case, that director should either not accept the position or abstain from the decision (explaining the reason) or should ask for consultancy with external experts (in case the decision is very technical or complex, for example). Finally, a distinction between the two categories of directors could be made by judges in case it is proven, under specific circumstances, that executive directors had some information not shared with nonexecutive directors (the "subjective test"). In addition, the subjective test can be applied whenever a director (either executive or nonexecutive) is an expert on a subject matter (e.g., a computer scientist dealing with a cybersecurity decision to be taken): in this case, courts may expect from such a director a higher level of expertise than could be expected from her/his peers.

Under *Section 175 CA*, directors have the duty to avoid conflicts of interest: if there are interests in the transactions or arrangements undertaken by the company, these must be notified to the other directors. The transaction or the arrangement can be carried out if authorized by the board of directors, provided that an interested director *does not take part in the decision (neither for reaching the quorum, nor for voting).*

A final source of directors' duty is the Insolvency Act 1986 with reference *to creditors*. When the company is insolvent, the duty to promote the success of the company is displaced, and creditors' interests shall be considered. *Section 214 of the Insolvency Act 1986* provides for liability for "wrongful trading," under which the liquidator can require the directors to contribute to the funds available to the creditors in an insolvent winding-up, as the court thinks proper, when they ought to have recognized that the company had no reasonable prospect of avoiding insolvent liquidation and then failed to take all the reasonable steps to minimize loss to the creditors.

5.7.1 Directors' Liabilities: Derivative Claims and Unfair Prejudice Remedy

In case directors breach one of the duties prescribed for them by the Companies Act, causing loss to the company's assets, who is eligible to sue the directors? What are the remedies granted to the shareholders?

The Companies Act does not vest the power to sue directors to a particular organ of the company; it is up to the articles of association to provide rules on this matter. Most articles of association assign to the board of directors the power to start a legal action as this is deemed a managerial decision.[26] However, the board of directors might have no motive to start a legal action against one or more of its members, and, of course, there is conflict of interest on the part of the directors. To prove this, as matter of fact, few legal suits have been brought against directors further to a resolution by the board of directors itself. Usually this occurred following a hostile takeovers when the legal suit was started by incumbent directors, or in case of a company's insolvency and liquidation when legitimacy is upon the commissioner or trustee who are in charge of the proceeding. However, case law has applied to legal suits against directors the general principle stating that the *general meeting of shareholders* can exercise reserved managerial power whenever the board of directors, for any reason, does not exercise such power; therefore, the general meeting of shareholders may start a legal suit against directors who breach their duties.[27] But, obviously, also the general meeting of shareholders may, directly or indirectly, be controlled or influenced by directors. That is why most jurisdictions also provide for legal remedies for individual or minority shareholders.

---

[26] Davies and Gower (2003), pp. 444–450.

[27] *Alexander Ward & Co Ltd v Samyang Navigation Co Ltd* [1975] 1 WLR 673, 679.

[28] *Foss v Harbottle* (1843), 2 Ha. 461, and *Mozley v Alston* (1847), 1 Ph. 790.

[29] *Foss v. Harbottle* has to be read in conjunction with *Prudential Assurance Co. Ltd. v. Newman Industries Ltd. and Others (No. 2)* [1982], Ch. 204, which denied individual members' legal action when the damage claimed consisted of mere reduction in share value, which reflects the loss suffered by the company's assets. The so-called reflective loss rule was later confirmed by *Johnson v. Gore, Wood & Co.* [2001] 1 All ER 481 (HL). However, in *Giles v. Rhind* [2002] EWCA Civ 1428, it was clarified that the latter rule does not apply, and a single shareholder may sue also for reflective damages if the defendant directors were those responsible for the company's economic conditions, depriving the company of the possibility to sue directors: in that case, the directors impoverished the company's assets to the level that it was left without resources even to start a legal proceeding.

The most important judicial remedy for individual shareholders is a *derivative action*. Prior to the Companies Act 2006, the circumstances in which a derivative action could be brought by shareholders were limited. In *Foss v. Harbottle*, it was held that where harm is done to a company, the proper claimant is the company itself, meaning the majority shareholders. This rule is a corollary of the legal personality of the company: duties are owed by the directors to the company, which is a separate legal person and is different from both directors and shareholders; therefore, individual members cannot have a cause of action for any damage incurred by the company which to sue directors shall comply with its internal organization rules.[28] The *Foss v Harbottle* rule, under which the proper plaintiff is the company and not any individual member, was applied very strictly by English courts.[29] It was as if the English judiciary was hit by an American phobia and was more worried of preventing any possible overdeterrence than avoiding underterrence in the English system.[30] The underlying assumption was that since shareholders hold small percentages of shares, their motive to bring an action to increase the company's assets should also be modest, unless additional questionable motives occur, such as to disturb management or to pursue personal or instrumental interests (so-called strike suits). A few cases started to provide for exceptions to the *Foss v Harbottle* rule, however. In *Wallersteiner v Moir (No. 2)*,[31] the derivative action was explicitly recognized and, with it, the principle according to which shareholders, even individually, may start a legal suit on behalf of the company against defaulting directors in case the latter were in control of the company. The exception to *Foss v Harbottle* was justified by the need to repair the injustice that would otherwise occur any time directors determine the company's conduct at the general meeting and at the board of directors making these two bodies failing to vote on a legal suit against directors themselves.[32] A derivative action is therefore a legal action that individual shareholders have the right to initiate on behalf of the company, and the relationship between the shareholders and the company qualifies as agency.[33] The consequence of this agency relationship is that legal costs incurred by the shareholders to start a

[30] The expression is by Howarth (1991), pp. 58, 66.

[31] [1975] Q.B. 373, 391 (CA). The Court developed two earlier cases: *East Pant Du United Lead Mining Co. Ltd. v Merryweather* (1864) 2 Hem. & M. 254 (even though limiting single shareholders' legitimacy to the evidence of fraudulent behavior from directors) and *Burland v Earle* [1902] A.C. 83 (according to which legitimacy could be recognized to a single shareholder representing herself/himself and other shareholders).

[32] Lord Denning in *Wallersteiner v. Moir (No. 2)*, p. 390, held: "In one way or another some means must be found for the company to sue. Otherwise the law would fail in its purpose. Injustice would be done without redress."

[33] Ibidem.

[34] Looking at the specific facts of the case in *Wallersteiner v. Moir*, the financial condition of the plaintiff shareholder was particularly difficult as he had spent all his resources in the lower courts to sue the director who had seriously breached various provisions; the plaintiff had tried to promote a legal action by the general meeting without success.

[35] *Wallersteiner v. Moir (No. 2)*, cit., 391–395.

legal proceeding should be borne by the company: since the plaintiff shareholders are the company's agents, the former have the right to be reimbursed by the company, who is the principal for all expenses incurred in the legal proceeding coherently with the general rule that is normally applied to agency.[34] It is explained in the *Wallersteiner* case that if the legal action is successful, damages will be paid by the directors to the company itself, and therefore, coherently, legal costs shall be borne by the company, which benefits from the legal action.[35] *Wallersteiner v. Moir (No. 2)* has been very important because it clarified, in particular, that if an individual member "reasonably and prudently" makes a decision to start a legal suit, which, given the specific circumstances, is in the interest of the company, that member cannot be held liable to pay legal costs, even in case the action is not successful: she/he is acting as plaintiff not for her/his own interest but for the company's interest, and therefore, legal costs shall be repaid to her/him, even if the legal suit is lost.[36] In order to ascertain the reasonableness and prudence of the legal suit from the company's viewpoint, *Wallersteiner v. Moir (No. 2)* introduced a procedural rule, taking inspiration from provisions on trust (where expenses incurred by the trustee on behalf of the trust fund shall be subject to reimbursement); under such rule, the plaintiff shareholder, in a derivative action, shall preliminarily ask the court to confirm the reasonableness of the case, and the court will discretionally decide whether to authorize the legal proceeding at the expense of the company; should the court not authorize the plaintiff to start the derivative suit, the plaintiff may do so, bearing the risk of paying the legal costs.

Later on, the Civil Procedure Rules (CPR), dated 1998, provided regulation for derivative actions, defined as actions brought "where a company, other incorporated body or trade union is alleged to be entitled to claim a remedy and a claim is made by one or more members of the company, body or trade union for it to be given that remedy" (CPR19.9(1)). According to these Rules, courts shall establish whether acknowledging reimbursement of legal costs to plaintiff if it is deemed proper (CPR 19.9(7)) and, in any case, express approval by courts to continue the action is required (CPR 19.9(3)). Under the same Rules, even just one member, regardless of the share capital threshold, may start a derivative action. This flexibility is balanced by the role played by courts, which is fundamental: judicial authorization is a prerequisite for starting a derivative action, and courts have the discretion whether to authorize it or not. In addition, courts have also powers to oversee the plaintiff's behavior and the entire proceeding as well as to authorize any settlement and shall assess whether legal costs have to be reimbursed by the company to the plaintiff.[37]

The result of the mentioned case law was a complex and often contradictory system of rules under which courts' approval was just one of the prerequisite to start a derivative action but additional conditions were introduced by different case law that made altogether almost impossible to start a derivative action. One of the

---

[36] Ibidem, 392.

[37] Davies and Gower (2003), p. 455.

most important provisions, introduced by the Companies Act in 2006, has been the regulation of the derivative action, was the introduction of with the aim to protect minority shareholders, by means of Sections 260 ff., in accordance with which even a single member, on behalf of the company, may apply to the courts to enforce any breach of directors' duties. Courts are given certain criteria for dismissing or authorizing a claim (the success of the company/authorization, ratification by members, lack of personal interest of the member); basically, the Court function is meant to select most meritorious cases. Courts' role is conceived as the necessary filter to prevent the system from spurious claims.

What about the legal costs incurred in suing defaulting directors? Who is going to pay them? Since shareholders are initiating a legal suit on behalf of the company, which in case of success would be the beneficiary of any payment made by the directors paying for damages, it should be coherent with logic and the original agency principles explained above that the company bears the legal costs. However, this is not the rule under the Companies Act: the court will decide who is going to bear the legal costs *if the claim is successful*. Therefore, minority shareholders who want to start a derivative claim against directors shall accept the risk of paying for the legal costs: if the case is not successful, they shall definitely pay the legal costs, but even if the claim is successful, they might be held responsible by the court to pay for legal damages. It can be easily understood that there are not many incentives for minority shareholders to start a derivative claim.

The procedure is very detailed under the Companies Act: Section 260 states that any member may seek relief on behalf of the company. A derivative claim may only be brought in respect of a cause of action arising from an actual or proposed act or omission involving negligence, default, breach of duty, or breach of trust by a director of the company. The cause of action may be against the director or another person (e.g., the company itself) or both. The procedure provides for two steps (Section 261 CA): a member of a company who brings a derivative claim *must apply to the court for permission to continue*; if it appears to the court that the application filed by the claimant and the evidence presented in support of it does not disclose a *prima facie case* for granting permission, the court must dismiss the application and may make any consequential order it considers appropriate. If the application is not dismissed, the court may give directions as to the evidence to be provided by the company and may adjourn the proceedings to enable evidence to be obtained. In hearing the application, the court may give permission (or leave) to continue the claim on such terms as it thinks fit or refuse permission and dismiss the claim or adjourn the proceedings on application and give such direction as it deems fit. Section 262 CA specifies that the application to the court for permission shall be commenced if the company has not initiated any other claim or has failed to prosecute the claim diligently, and in both cases, it is appropriate for the member to continue the claim as a derivative claim. Section 263 states that permission *must be refused* if the court is satisfied that a person acting in accordance with Section 172 (duty to promote the success of the company) would not seek to continue the claim or where the act or omission was authorized by the company before it occurred or has been ratified by the company since it occurred. The court must take into account, in particular, whether the member is acting in good faith in seeking to continue the claim; the importance that a person acting in accordance with Section 172 (duty to promote the success of the company) would attach to the act of continuing it; whether the cause of action results from an act or omission that is yet to occur, whether the act or omission could be, and in the circumstances would likely be, authorized by the company before it occurs or ratified by the company after it occurs; whether the company has decided not to pursue the claim; whether the act or omission in respect of which the claim is brought gives rise to a cause of action that the member could pursue in her/his own right rather than on behalf of the company. In considering whether to give permission (or leave), the court shall have particular regard *to any evidence* before it concerning the views of the members of the company who have no personal interest, direct or indirect, in the matter.

If all these conditions are met, the shareholder may start the derivative claim on behalf of the company.

Another remedy that is typical of the UK legal system only (as many jurisdictions in the world recognize derivative claims) is the *unfair prejudice remedy*. Section 994 CA states that a shareholder may file a petition for relief where the company's affairs are being or have been conducted in a manner that is unfairly prejudicial to the interests of the petitioner. The provision is wide indeed because it does not specify who the defendant is: it can be the company itself, the directors, or the majority shareholders. In addition, the provision does not specify the remedy: the petitioner may ask for damages or for any order from the court. Coherently, courts have extensive remedial powers; the most common remedy is to order the oppressors (i.e., the majority shareholders) to purchase the shares of the minority at fair market value.

5.7.2 Leading Cases on Directors' Liability

One of the few cases dealing with the enforcement of Section 172 CA is *People & Planet v. HM Treasury*.

People & Planet v. HM Treasury[38]

People and Planet (the most important student organization in the UK for the protection of human rights and the environment etc.) filed a legal suit against HM Treasury, which holds 70% of shares in Royal Bank of Scotland (RBS)—through UK Financial Investment Ltd.—claiming its lack of adequate environmental and human rights considerations in investing in RBS. RBS has allegedly used public monies to finance several controversial companies and projects that undermined the UK's commitment to halt climate change. The plaintiff claimed that RBS undertook activities toward clients that were not in compliance with the need to protect the environment and human rights. The issue at stake was how to manage (through financing and loans) the shareholding in RBS—under a commercial approach or with a view to protecting the environment and human rights? HM Treasury's defense was that the recapitalization of the bank was decided for the management of RBS with a view to maximizing profits for the benefit of British taxpayers,

(continued)

[38] [2009] EWHC 3020 (Admin).

therefore according to a commercial approach. However, HM Treasury added that RBS "will of course take into account the extent to which the investee companies' corporate social responsibility policies will benefit the investee companies and therefore their shareholders" and "will expect the investee companies to pursue responsible policies with regard to environmental issues and human rights, because of the negative implications—reputational, regulatory and other, which all affect the value of the company—for any company and its shareholders for not doing so." If proven that RBS's policy on corporate social responsibility was worse than other banks', to undermine RBS's reputation compared to other peers and consequently its shareholder value, the government, as a shareholder, would therefore intervene to correct the management.

The High Court of Justice denied the request for permission to hold a judicial review over the Treasury's actions, holding that social and environmental issues may be taken into consideration by RBS directors *only within the context of duties imposed to them by Sec. 172 CA 2006*. So the action brought by People and Planet was rejected. If RBS directors try to pursue social or environmental issues beyond what is allowed under Section 172, they would breach the provision and would be liable to pay damages in case of a decrease in the company's assets consequent to such decisions.

Therefore, under Section 172, stakeholders' interests may be taken into consideration by directors only instrumentally, in so far as they contribute to the increase of shareholder value. However, in shareholder value, also reputation, regulatory consequences, etc. are included. If directors pursue stakeholders' interests without considering that their primary duty is toward the company—meant as shareholders as a whole—they breach Section 172 and are therefore liable to pay damages occurring to the company's assets. This case represents the best explanation of what "enlightened shareholder value" means in practice.

Another case worth mentioning in relation to Section 172 CA is *ClientEarth v. Shell Plc*.

ClientEarth v. Shell Plc.[39]

ClientEarth is an environmental law charity holding shares in Shell plc. A derivative action was brought by ClientEarth, seeking permission to bring a claim on the ground that the directors were fundamentally mismanaging climate risk, thereby being in breach of their legal duties under Section 172 CA (duty to promote the success of the company) and Section 174 CA (duty to exercise reasonable care, skill, and diligence). The remedies requested were a declaration that the directors are in breach of their duties and an order that the directors prepare and adopt a strategy that includes GHG reduction targets aligned with the goals of the Paris Agreement. Shell had adopted a strategic plan to reduce GHG emissions. However, it was argued by ClientEarth that this plan was not adequate and was inconsistent with decarbonization and the net-zero transition for the following very specific reasons: no short-term absolute emission reduction targets were considered; the medium-term (in 2030) absolute emission reduction target excluded scope 3 (indirect) emissions, while scope 1 (direct emissions) and scope 2 (electricity used) comprise less than 10% of the company's total footprint—this means that more than 90% of the emissions from which the company derives revenue are excluded from its only interim absolute emission reduction target; Shell's interim intensity targets are extremely low (e.g., 20% carbon intensity reduction by 2030 equates to merely 3% of its absolute emissions in 2020); Shell relies heavily on offsets, which would require an unrealistic amount of land to realize (approximately the size of the UK); Shell intends to grow its gas and oil business, which is contradictory with the policy of GHG reduction; and there is no real diversification into renewables/low-carbon technologies.

The High Court of Justice denied the *prima facie* case and, therefore, the authorization to file a derivative action, holding that, with reference to the mismanagement of climate risk, the

(continued)

[39] [2023] EWHC 1137 (Ch).

obligations pleaded by ClientEarth to be complied by the directors are too specific, and this is in contrast with the rule according to which it is upon the directors to "determine (acting in good faith) how to best promote the success of the company for the benefit of its members as whole." The weighing of all considerations set out under Section 172 CA is essentially "a commercial decision which the court is ill-equipped to take." In addition, Section 174 CA "does not superimpose on that duty more specific obligations as to what is and is not reasonable in every circumstance." The High Court explained that the way in which ClientEarth puts its case seeks to impose absolute duties on the directors, which cut across their general duty to have regard to the many competing considerations as to how best to promote the success of Shell for the benefit of its members as a whole. The impact of Shell's operations on the community and the environment is a matter that the directors are required to weigh in the balance. In addition, the High Court was not satisfied that ClientEarth was acting in good faith, a situation that will count strongly against a conclusion that it has established a *prima facie* case for permission: being a holder of only 27 shares in Shell, it has not adduced sufficient evidence to counter the inference of collateral motive to bring the action as its real interest is not in how best to promote the success of Shell for the benefit of its members as a whole. Finally, the High Court also considered that at Shell's annual general meeting, the support for its strategic climate plan from the shareholders was 88.4% of the votes; the strength of the members' support for the directors' strategic approach to climate change risk is a factor to which the court is bound to have particular regard if faced with a substantive application for permission. The decision has been appealed by ClientEarth.
This is a very important decision in climate change litigation because it has been the first one worldwide addressing a legal suit for climate risk mismanagement brought against a company's directors personally; previous cases, concerning the climate, were brought against companies or states.

Another case to be mentioned that is in between a derivative action and an unfair prejudice remedy is *Franbar Holdings Ltd. v Patel.*

Franbar Holdings Ltd. v Patel[40]

The share capital of the company Medicentres was divided between Franbar Holdings Ltd., owning 25% of shares, and Casualty Plus Ltd., owning 75%. The two shareholders entered into a shareholder agreement, according to which Franbar had the right to appoint two directors, while Casualty had the right to appoint three directors (including the chairman). Franbar brought both a derivative claim (asking for permission from the court) and an unfair prejudice remedy under Section 996 of the Companies Act, complaining that the directors appointed by Casualty had diverted business opportunities from Medicentres to Casualty Plus; one of the directors appointed by Franbar was suspended despite his skills and expertise (but the defense alleged that misconduct justified the suspension); there was failure to provide adequate financial information (but the defense claimed that all directors should have been responsible for that and not only those appointed by Casualty); one of the directors appointed by Casualty was unfit to be director and misused company assets, and the other directors and Casualty itself knew about it (but the defense claimed this was not true); and other miscellaneous reasons, such as valuable contracts lost, negligence in negotiations for a leasing agreement, etc. (but the defense claimed this was not true). The claimant sought a derivative action (Section 260 CA) or an unfair prejudice remedy (Section 994 CA) or a breach of the shareholder agreement (but the same substantive allegations were filed) and the indemnification of costs by the company in the case of success. The relief that is primarily sought from the Court was an order against Casualty Plus to purchase Franbar's shares in Medicentres at a fair price, to be determined. The Court did not reach any conclusion on the merit of the dispute. The Court started by examining the existence of a *prima facie* case for a

(continued)

[40] [2008] EWHC 1534 (Ch).

derivative action in accordance with Section 260 CA as Franbar brought the claim on behalf of the company, Medicentres, against its directors.
The Court evaluated the case using various tests: first, whether the claim arises "from an actual or proposed act or omission involving negligence, default, breach of duty or breach of trust by a director of the company." The power of the Court is defined under Section 261 (4) CA: "On hearing the application, the court may: (a) Give permission (or leave) to continue the claim on such terms as it thinks fit, (b) refuse permission (or leave) and dismiss the claim, or (c) adjourn the proceedings on the application and give such directions as it thinks fit."
Under which criterion the claim is considered? Section 263 CA explains that the Court shall consider what a hypothetical director, in good faith, would do under Section 172 CA to promote the success of the company in those circumstances. Would she/he *seek to continue* the claim or not? According to the Court, this was one of those cases in which there is room for more than one view, but there is sufficient material for the hypothetical director to conclude that the conduct of Medicentres' business by those in control of it had given rise to actionable breaches of duty, and the two directors appointed by Casualty were behind much of that conduct. So the judge stated: "I cannot be satisfied that a hypothetical director, acting in accordance with Section 172, would conclude that the case advanced was insufficiently cogent to justify continuation of the claim. Even though he may take a healthily skeptical approach to Medicentres' ability to prove the allegations at trial, it does not follow that the claim should not be continued on that ground alone."
The second test, required by the Companies Act, is whether the claimant is in good faith. Though the alternative remedy for Mr. Franbar, the buyout of shares, was more relevant, the judged believed "it is difficult to say he is not in good faith," adding that "I am not satisfied that Franbar has any motive in wishing to continue the derivative claim, apart from a desire to ensure that the value it extracts from its shareholding in Medicentres is full and fair. Furthermore, even though the offer made by Casualty Plus has not been accepted, it is not clear that it was in such a form that its refusal could be said to evidence a lack of good faith. I cannot say at this stage that it is not being pursued in good faith." It is interesting to refer to all the considerations made by the judge in that case to understand the way of reasoning of English courts. So with reference to the question of whether a hypothetical director would *continue* the claim or not, the judgment was that "the hypothetical director acting in accordance with Section 172 would take into account a wide range of considerations when assessing the importance of continuing the claim. These would include such matters as the prospects of success of the claim, the ability of the company to make a recovery on any award of damages, the disruption which would be caused to the development of the company's business by having to concentrate on the proceedings, the costs of the proceedings and any damage to the company's reputation and business if the proceedings were to fail. A director will often be in the position of having to make what is no more than a partially informed decision on continuation without any very clear idea of how the proceedings might turn out. In my judgment, the difficulty with this submission is that the complaints are not yet in a form in which the hypothetical director might be expected to conclude that there were obvious breaches of duty which ought to be pursued and that the recovery to be expected in consequence of those breaches would be substantial. I also think that it is likely that the hypothetical director would be more inclined to regard pursuit of the derivative claim as less important in the light of the fact that several of the complaints are more naturally to be formulated as breaches of the Shareholders' Agreement and acts of unfair prejudice which are already the subject matter of proceedings commenced by the minority shareholder," accepting that "in the present case, where all parties seek and have offered (as the case may be) a buy-out of the minority by the majority and the principal issue is one of valuation, that means that the hypothetical director would be less likely to attribute importance to the continuation of the derivative claim." In other words, absent any obvious breaches of duty, the buyout of minority and valuation of shares were more important in that case than a derivative claim. Another consideration to be made by courts with reference to derivative actions is whether there was or there might be ratification by Medicentres of acts of directors performed by connected persons. The judge believed that because persons connected to the directors are involved, some of the complaints made by Franbar may well be *incapable of*

(continued)

ratification. The judge believed that "most of the allegations of breach of duty to Medicentres (and certainly all those which are even arguably incapable of ratification) are likely to be relevant to Franbar's complaint of unfair prejudice. Furthermore, the losses which Medicentres might have sustained as a result of the breaches of duty pleaded in the derivative claim are relevant to the fair value of Franbar's shares and to the question of what factual assumptions should be made on the valuation to ensure that Franbar is put into the position that it would have been in but for the unfair prejudice which it will (on this hypothesis) have established. I can see no reason why Franbar should not be granted such relief on the unfair prejudice petition as may be necessary to ensure that the interest which it seeks to realize is valued on a basis which takes full account of the value of the complaints it wishes to pursue on behalf of Medicentres in the derivative claim." Which was presumably the real concern of Franbar? In the end, it was clear that Franbar's real concern was that Casualty Plus might not be in a position to pay a fair value for Franbar's shares in Medicentres (having regard to the value of Medicentres' claims against Mr. Patel and Dr. du Plessis), while a judgment against the two directors personally was one more likely to be satisfied by them.. In the end, while permission to continue a derivative claim was not granted given the circumstances of the case, the unfair prejudice remedy was granted. All parties and the Court accepted at the end that the proper ambit of this dispute was about the terms on which Franbar could exit from Medicentres; it was not a case in which there was any question that a remedy was required to protect the interests of a minority shareholder wishing to remain involved in Medicentres' affairs. The judge held that "Franbar should be able to achieve all that it can properly want through the Section 994 petition and the shareholders' action. Having regard to all of these considerations, and carrying out the balancing exercise as best I can on the information currently available, it is my judgment that justice is best achieved by refusing permission to continue."

5.8 Institutional Investors

As explained under Section 5.2, given the ownership pattern in the UK, the presence of institutional investors is highly important. A code of conduct, the Stewardship Code, was adopted in 2020 addressing institutional investors in order to foster their responsible participation in listed companies. By stewardship is meant the "Responsible allocation, management and oversight of capital to create long-term value for clients and beneficiaries leading to sustainable benefits for the economy, the environment and society." Addressees of the Code are asset owners and asset managers, who together reach a majority of share capital, on average, in the UK financial market. It is a code of conduct, that is, a soft law, and is therefore not binding. However, its effectiveness is encouraged by the rule "apply or explain," which requires institutional investors to adopt the spirit of the code more comprehensively or explain why they depart from it. It has been beautifully explained that "stewardship does not merely serve investment priorities but denotes a wider social need to address a collective action problem."[41] This new edition of the Code reflects the general view that stewardship can no longer be seen under a merely financially oriented investment lens since it spreads across a wide range of issues, which are

[41] Sergakis (2023), p. 11.

[42] Ibidem, p. 3.

nowadays also captured by considering environmental, social, and governance (ESG) factors.[42] These factors are expressly mentioned in the UK Stewardship Code.

Principles 1 to 5 concern Purpose and Governance; Principles 6 to 8 refer to the Investment Approach; Principles 9 to 11 are on Engagement, and Principle 12 is about Rights and Responsibilities.

The 2020 edition of the Code focuses on environmental, particularly climate change, and social factors, in addition to governance, which have become material issues for investors to consider when making investment decisions and undertaking stewardship. The Code also recognizes that asset owners and asset managers play an important role as guardians of market integrity and in working to minimize systemic risks as well as being stewards of the investments in their portfolios.

The main provisions provide that institutional investors should identify and disclose:

1. The *purpose* of the organization (i.e., culture, values, business model, strategy) as well as their investment beliefs (what factors they consider important for desired investment outcomes and why, what actions they have taken, and how effective they have been)
2. The *governance structure*, i.e., processes to enable oversight and accountability for effective stewardship (i.e., organization, qualifications of workforce, research, etc.), investigating how effective they are and if they can be improved, and specifying what actions they have taken as well as how effective they have been
3. *Conflicts of interests*, specifying the policy adopted to identify and manage actual and potential conflicts related to stewardship (examples of conflicts of interests may derive from ownership structure, business relations, cross-directorships, client/beneficiary interests diverging from each other, etc.)
4. *Market-wide and systemic risks* (for which after identification, assessment, and solutions, work with other stakeholders shall be explained, e.g., change in interest rates, geopolitical issues, currency rate, climate change, pandemics, etc.)
5. *Policies* to ensure effective stewardship (explaining how they have ensured that stewardship reporting is fair, balanced, and understandable, e.g., through a designated body, internal auditor, independent third party, internal committee, etc.)
6. Clients' and beneficiaries' needs in terms of *investment approach* (what they are, how they are sought, etc.)
7. *Issues prioritized* for assessing investments, holding, and exit, including environmental, social, and governance (ESG) issues
8. *Monitoring* of service providers (i.e., asset managers, investment consultants, proxy advisors, data and research providers) to ensure that services have been delivered to meet their needs
9. *Engagement*, specifying the methods for choosing (i.e., the key issues or the size of holdings), the reasons for such approach, the differences for funds, geographies, etc. (examples of engagement are meeting the chairman or the

chief executive officers or other board members, holding meetings with the management, writing letters, raising key issues through company advisers, etc.)

10. *Collaborative engagement with other investors* to motivate an issuer to achieve a certain result (e.g., working in coalition with certain investors or with wider stakeholders, etc.)
11. How they decide on *escalation* (i.e., buy, sell, hold), explaining which priorities they have (issues, reasons, funds/assets/geographies)
12. Active *exercise of rights and responsibilities*, such as voting policy, rational of voting decisions (e.g., pro/against the board, withholding, the use of recommendations by proxy advisors, direct voting by clients, etc.), seeking access to information, etc.

References

Bebchuk LA, Tallarita R (2020) The illusory promise of stakeholder governance. Cornell Law Rev 106:91–177

Blair T (1998) The third way. Fabian Society, London

Bruno S (2004) Profili di diritto societario inglese alla luce della riforma. Rivista delle società:897–961

Bruno S (2012) Directors' versus shareholders' primacy in U.S. Corporations through the eyes of history: Is directors' power "inherent"? Eur Company Financ Rev 9(4):421–445

Bruno S (2017) The 'enlightened shareholder value' in UK companies ten years later: What the European Directive N. 2014/95/EC can do. In: Le droit compare des affaires au XXI siècle. Mélanges à la mémoire de Claude Ducouloux-Favard. Bruylant, Bruxelles, p 315

Davies P (2002) Introduction to company law. Oxford University Press, Oxford

Davies PL, Gower LCB (2003) Gower & Davies' principles of modern company law, 7th edn. Thomson – Sweet & Maxwell, London

Dean J (2001) Directing public companies: Company law and the stakeholder society. Routledge/Cavendish, London/Sidney

Giddens A (1998) The third way. Polity Press, Cambridge

Higgs D (2003) Review of the role and effectiveness of non-executive directors, at http://www.dti.gov.uk/cld/non_exec_review

Howarth D (1991) Negligence after Murphy: time to rethink. Camb Law J 50(1):58–99

Keay A (2010) The duty to promote the success of the company: is it fit for purpose?, at www.law.leeds.ac.uk/assets/files/research/events/directors-duties/keay-the-duty-to-promote-the-success.pdf

Kelly G, Parkinson J (1998) The conceptual foundations of the company: a pluralist approach. Comp Financ Insolvency Law Rev 2:174–197

Lowry J (2009) The duty of loyalty of company directors: bridging the accountability gap through efficient disclosure. Camb Law J 68(3):607–622

Mazzuccato M (2018) The value of everything. Making and taking in the global economy. Allen Lane, Great Britain

Parkinson J (2002) Inclusive company law. In: De Lacy J (ed) The reform of United Kingdom company law. Routledge/Cavendish, London/Sidney, p 43

Roach L (2001) The paradox of the traditional justification for exclusive shareholder governance protection: expanding the pluralist approach. Comp Lawy 22(9):12

Sergakis K (2023) Shareholder stewardship: autonomy and sociality. J Corp Law Stud 23(2): 497–535. https://doi.org/10.1080/14735970.2023.2294550

Wheeler S (2002) Corporations & the third way. Hart Publisher, Oxford/Portland

European Company Law: Special Focus on Italian Company Law

6

Contents

6.1 Introduction to European Company Law: Sources of European Company Law

The legal basis for the harmonization of company law is Article 50 of the Treaty on the Functioning of the European Union, according to which:

> In order to attain freedom of establishment as regards a particular activity, the European Parliament and the Council, acting in accordance with the ordinary legislative procedure and after consulting the Economic and Social Committee, shall act by means of *directives*.[1]

[1] Consolidated Version C 202/68 of 7 June 2016.

S. Bruno, *Foundations of Business and Company Law*,
https://doi.org/10.1007/978-3-031-71885-4_6

Article 288 of the same Treaty explains:

> To exercise the Union's competences, the institutions shall adopt regulations, directives, decisions, recommendations and opinions. A *regulation* shall have general application. It shall be binding in its entirety and directly applicable in all Member States. A *directive* shall be binding, as to the result to be achieved, upon each Member State to which it is addressed, but shall leave to the national authorities the choice of form and methods. A *decision* shall be binding in its entirety. A *decision* which specifies those to whom it is addressed shall be binding only on them. *Recommendations* and *opinions* shall have no binding force.

Therefore, with reference to directives, it is up to member states to devise their own laws to reach the goals set therein. However, if a directive is adequately detailed in its provisions, so as to eliminate any discretion from member states, so-called *self-executing directive* (as it happens in some more recent directives), it is said that it does not require any implementation from member states and can be applied directly toward citizens in case a member state has not (yet) implemented the directive.

6.2 Harmonization of European Company Law

Article 50 of the Treaty on the Functioning of the European Union, mentioned in the previous paragraph, was a clear instruction to harmonize basic rules of national company law systems, that is, rules on public and private companies, launching a very ambitious program for that purpose.[2]

Accordingly, the *First Company Law Directive* (N. 68/151/EEC) covered all limited liability companies (private and public companies) to deal with:

1. The disclosure of company documents when a private or public company is incorporated
2. The validity of obligations entered into by a company; and
3. Nullity

Its main aim is to protect third parties that negotiate with a private or public company. Therefore, the basic documents of incorporation (articles of association and bylaws) shall be disclosed:

> in order that third parties may be able to ascertain their contents and other information concerning the company, especially particulars of the persons who are authorized to bind the company.[3]

[2]Timmermans (2003), pp. 623–630.

[3]See Whereas n. 4) of First Council Directive N. 68/151/EEC.

All interested parties may obtain from the register (documenting the incorporation) a copy of such documents and particulars by paper as well as by electronic means. In addition, the protection of third parties is ensured by those provisions that limit the grounds on which the obligations entered into in the name of the company are not valid. Finally, with the aim of ensuring legal certainty on relations between the company and third parties, as well as among members, the cases in which nullity of acts can arise are restricted; for the same reason also, the retroactive effect of a declaration of nullity is avoided, and any such declaration does produce effects only from the date of declaration onward.

However, the original ambition, after the First Directive, was downgraded, and priority was given to the harmonization of public companies but with the intention, once the harmonization of public companies was completed, to continue the harmonization of private companies even though this aspiration has not materialized.[4] The *Second Company Law Directive* (N. 77/91/EEC, replaced by Directive 2017/1132/EU) refers to public companies limited by shares only. The aim is to protect the interests of both shareholders and creditors by:

1. Regulating the maintenance of share capital by setting the minimum share capital at €25,000, and
2. Prohibiting any reduction thereof "by distribution to shareholders where the latter are not entitled to it and by imposing limits on the company's right to acquire its own shares as well as on the financial assistance on a company's own shares"

It also provides for the principle of equal treatment for all shareholders who are in the same position. Likewise, the *Third Company Law Directive* (N. 78/855/EEC) was enacted to regulate only public companies with reference to mergers, followed by the *Eleventh Directive* (N. 89/666/EEC) on splitting (demergers). The *Fourth* (N. 78/660/EEC) and *Seventh Company Law Directives* (N. 83/349/EEC, as amended most recently by Directive N. 2013/34/EU) address annual financial statements and directors' reports, including consolidated accounts, and they apply to both public and private companies. The financial statements comprise:

1. The balance sheet, setting forth on an annual basis the assets and liabilities of the company
2. The profit and loss account, setting forth on an annual basis the income and expenditure of the company and the resulting profit or loss actually made, and
3. The notes to the accounts indicating the valuation criteria adopted for each item in the financial statements as well as any other information required by law

Finally, the financial statements must be accompanied by a directors' report on the company's performance during the relative financial year. Financial statements are an essential characteristic of companies in that they provide both members and

[4] Timmermans (2003), pp. 623–630.

third parties with information regarding the economic and financial state of the company and serve to document the position of members (for example, shares and voting rights are measured by reference to the share capital, as are dividend rights, preemption rights, and so forth) and allow those that intend to contract with the company to be aware of its financial state. The latter Directives were completed by the *Eleventh Directive* (N. 89/666/EC), concerning disclosure requirements in respect of branches opened in a member state by certain types of companies governed by the law of another state.

However, the harmonization of private companies has not been achieved as yet: only the *Twelfth Directive* (N. 89/667/EEC, as amended by Directive 2009/102/EEC) that regulates the one-member private company can be mentioned in addition to those above mentioned.

The *Fifth Directive*, which should have been adopted to regulate corporate governance (on the powers, structure, and obligations of the organs of public companies), never came to light, with the result that there are different models of corporate governance, namely, different models of boards and internal control among jurisdictions, as will be analyzed below (see Section 6.3).[5] The *Ninth Company Law Directive* is still a Draft Proposal and refers to a group of companies firstly produced in 1980.

Another directive to be mentioned, addressing listed companies exclusively, is Directive N. 2007/36/EC, as modified by Directives N. 2014/59/EU and N. 2017/838/EU on *shareholders' rights*, aiming at fostering the voice of shareholders in general meetings of listed companies and, more precisely, the exercise of cross-border voting rights, engagement and disclosure for institutional investors and asset managers with reference to the exercise of their voting rights, and shareholders' vote on the remuneration of executive directors as well as on related-party transactions. These Directives have introduced a new focus on general meetings to increase good corporate governance and to balance the powers of both controlling shareholders and managers. Provisions on the following issues were introduced:

1. Attendance of general meetings via electronic means and cross-border voting
2. Casting of informed votes and, therefore, timely information (through electronic means and on Internet sites)
3. Shareholders' right to initiate general meetings and to pose questions on items on the agenda and to have answers from the issuer
4. Abolition of any restriction on voting other than what is necessary to identify shareholders
5. Deregulation of solicitation of proxy voting

The rationale is that voting rights shall be exercised since they are reflected in the price paid at the acquisition of shares, also considering that effective shareholder

[5] The Proposal, originally dated 1972, was amended in 1983 and 1991 and was finally withdrawn by the European Commission in 2001.

control is a prerequisite of sound corporate governance. With reference to cross-border voting rights, these Directives have reflected the fact that globalization also meant that significant proportions of shares in listed companies are held by foreign shareholders (in all countries, foreign institutional investors own much more than domestic ones), and therefore, voting must be facilitated. As a result of these Directives, attendance at general meetings and voting have sharply increased in European-listed companies.

Some of the abovementioned Directives and provisions have been combined and codified into Directive N. 2017/1132/EU.

Since Directive N. 2014/95/EU (*Non-Financial Reporting Directive*), harmonization has also covered sustainability issues by providing for disclosure from large undertakings (i.e., listed companies with over 500 employees, banks, insurance and reinsurance companies) on policies pursued by the company with reference to environmental, social, governance (so-called ESG), and diversity issues. Those companies were obliged not to pursue policies addressing ESG and diversity factors but only to declare whether they are pursued, justifying any choice not to pursue them. However, the underlying strategy of the European legislature has been to trigger, because of disclosure and subsequent judgment by the market, consideration of those factors in planning the company's activity. The non-financial reporting Directive has been replaced by Directive N. 2022/2464/EU (*Corporate Sustainability Reporting Directive (CSRD)*), which addresses a larger number of undertakings, that is, big sized companies (as defined) and all listed companies, including medium- and small-sized companies, with the exception of microenterprises, which are defined as "public interest entities" under Article 2), n. 1, lett. a) of the Directive, which also include banks and insurance companies. Directive N. 2022/2464/EU was enacted, together with Commission Delegated Regulation N. 2023/2772/EU, as regards sustainability reporting standards. Under the new rules, information to be published in the sustainability report has been standardized: five standards refer to climate change, the environment, and biodiversity; four standards refer to social issues; and one standard refers to governance. Undertakings may avoid disclosure on ESG policies only if they explain why those factors are not material for the company's activity, business model, and position; however, if disclosure refers to climate change, justification of its omission shall be given in detail. Particular focus is devoted to climate change, and companies are obliged to adopt energy transition plans, including implementing actions and related financial and investment plans, to ensure that their business model and strategy are aligned with:

1. The transition to a sustainable economy
2. The limiting of global warming to 1.5 °C in line with the Paris Agreement (i.e., not exceeding 1.5 °C increase of temperature by the end of the century)
3. The objective of achieving climate neutrality by 2050, as established by Regulation N. 2021/1119/EU[6]

[6]See Article 19-*bis,* para. 2, lett. a), iii, of Directive N. 2022/2464/EU.

In addition, companies are required to describe:

1. The absolute greenhouse gas emission reduction targets at least for 2030 and 2050
2. The progress made toward achieving those targets
3. A statement of whether those targets are based on conclusive scientific evidence[7]

Moreover, the sustainability reporting standards shall specify climate change mitigation targets, including as regards Scope 1, Scope 2, and Scope 3 greenhouse gas emissions.[8] Finally, companies shall also disclose plans of mitigation and adaptation to climate change.[9]

Moreover, with reference to listed companies solely, European Directive N. 2022/2381/EU on Improving the *Gender Balance Among Directors of Listed Companies* and Related Measures (so-called Women on Boards Directive) has been enacted. This Directive aims to achieve a more balanced representation between women and men among the directors of listed companies by establishing effective measures that aim to accelerate progress toward gender balance while allowing listed companies sufficient time to make the necessary arrangements for that purpose. Under it, by July 2026, all big publicly listed companies in the EU will have to take measures to increase women's presence at their helm so that at least 40% of nonexecutive director posts or 33% of all director (executive and nonexecutive) posts are occupied by the underrepresented sex by the end of July 2026. Merit must remain the key criterion in selection procedures, which should be transparent; listed companies will have to provide information about the gender representation on their boards to the competent authorities once a year and, if the objectives have not been met, how they plan to attain them. This information will be published on the company's website in an easily accessible manner. Penalties are left to member states that need to put in place rules on effective, dissuasive, and proportionate measures, such as fines, for companies that fail to comply with open and transparent appointment procedures. A judicial body could also annul the board of directors selected by the company if it breaches the principles of the Directive.

Additionally, the *Corporate Sustainability Due Diligence Directive (CS3D)* N. 2024/1760/EU has been approved by the European Council and Parliament. It requires firms and their upstream and downstream partners, including supply, production, and distribution partners, to prevent, end, or mitigate their adverse impact on human rights and the environment. Such impacts will include slavery, child labor, labor exploitation, biodiversity loss, pollution, or destruction of natural heritage. In particular, the firms involved are:

---

[7] See Article 19-bis, para. 2 lett. b), ivi.

[8] See Article 29b, para. 2, lett. a), i), ivi.

[9] See Requirement E1–2—Policies related to climate change mitigation and adaptation of Regulation N. 2023/2772/EU.

1. EU companies and parent companies with over 1000 employees and a net worldwide turnover higher than 450 million euros
2. Companies with franchising or licensing agreements in the EU ensuring a common corporate identity with a worldwide turnover higher than 80 million euros if at least 22.5 million euros were generated by royalties
3. Non-EU companies and parent companies with a net turnover of more than 450 million euros generated in Europe and companies with franchising or licensing agreements in the EU where those agreements ensure a common identity and those royalties amounted to more than 22.5 million euros and reaching a net turnover of more than 80 million euros generated in the EU.

These companies are basically required to integrate due diligence processes into their policies, make related investments, seek contractual assurances from their partners, improve their business plan, or provide support to small and medium-sized business partners in order to ensure that they comply with the mentioned obligations. The CS3D is a milestone for responsible business conduct aiming at halting the exploitation of people and the planet by companies.

Finally, in terms of harmonization, it has to be mentioned Regulation N. 2157/2001, which introduced the *Societas Europaea (SE)*. It is a type of public company that adds to the other types existing in each jurisdiction. SE can be incorporated in any of the member states and can operate everywhere in Europe: rules for SE are basically the same in all member states, with a few distinctions, as some of the provisions leave discretion on certain issues (mainly on boards' models) to shareholders.

6.3 Lack of Harmonization in Europe with Reference to Corporate Governance: Different Models of Boards in Public Companies Limited by Shares

Historically, as already mentioned in Section 4.1, the original model of a company limited by shares was born in Great Britain and had a one-tier structure: the East India Company, which originated in 1600 and whose sole governing body was elected by a general assembly of shareholders.[10] Its accounts and register of all goods were kept by one or more *Pursers*, who were appointed by the governor and the general assembly; the accounts were certified by external auditors, appointed by the general assembly and therefore laid down before the general assembly.[11] Nowadays the internal organization, i.e. the governance structure, of companies is not changed in United Kingdom: the Joint Stock Companies Act dated 1844 and the subsequent changes and consolidations brought to statutory company law—that

[10] Cf. the Charter granted by Queen Elizabeth, founding the company, 31 December 1600 (1893), pp. 163, 168 ss. See Section 4.1 above.

[11] Stevens (1886), pp. 41–45, 297–300.

have resulted in the Companies Acts of 1908, 1929, 1948, 1985, 1989, and finally 2006 currently in force—see the general meeting of shareholders appointing the board of directors; no other internal body is provided neither under the legislation, nor according to practice as explained under Section 5.6 while the company's accounts are certified by external auditors appointed by the general meeting. The alternative board model, the *Verenigde OostIndische Compagnie* (VOC), analyzed in this chapter, emerged in 1602 in the Netherlands and could be considered a predecessor of the two-tier board model: the six Chambers in port cities used to appoint delegates, the *college van heren*, that exercised a certain degree of supervision over the 60 executives (*bewindhebbers*) and therefore two bodies started to appear in the governance structure. However, it was not a real two-tier board until 1770, when supervisory board members became more common, which had the task of controlling accounts, determining dividends, discharging directors, and sometimes also deciding on policies.[12]

It was the one-tier British model that later on, during the nineteenth century, inspired the French Code of 1804 and, through it, the subsequent pieces of legislation adopted by other European states.[13]

During the nineteenth century in Europe, as companies started operating in more and more complex businesses and shares were subscribed by people very often living far from the company's office, shareholders felt the need to exercise autonomous supervision over the conduct of the company's affairs, and therefore over the directors, and *voluntarily* started to appoint a permanent supervisory body, in addition to the board of directors. Many big companies in France and Italy started to insert in their articles of association clauses providing for the appointment of such a body through a general meeting of shareholders, even when government supervision was granted by legislation.[14] Some European legislation started to provide for the *possibility* of appointing such internal bodies: the Dutch Code 1838 used to mention both directors and commissioners (*Commissarissen*) in companies limited by shares (Articles 43 and 52), and the German Code (before the Law dated 11th June 1870 was issued) used to mention the possibility of a supervisory board (*Aufrichtsrath*) in companies limited by shares (Article 223). At the same time, British law, in the Companies Act 1862, All. 1 Sample of Articles of Association, Sections 83–94, provided, as a default rule, that companies *could* have one or more auditors, shareholders, or nonshareholders, appointed the first time by directors and subsequently in the annual general meeting of stockholders or, upon the request of at least five shareholders, by the Ministry of Trade, having the task of examining, at least once a year, the company's accounts and ascertaining the correctness of

---

[12] O' Donnell (1952), pp. 55–60.

[13] Troplong (1845), who wrote that the French Napoleon Code, in regulating *societè anonyme*, "did not invent anything"; "it just copied" the British model, originated by the East India Company, as this "was the best thing to do."

[14] Relazione del Ministro di Grazia e Giustizia e dei Culti (Mancini) od Esposizione dei Motivi del Progetto del Codice di Commercio pel Regno d'Italia (1878), pp. 404–410.

financial statements; the power to inspect companies' books and accounts; and the duty to submit an annual report before the general meeting of stockholders. In France, however, Law 24th July 1867 (the first piece of legislation to regulate companies limited by shares after the Commercial Code 1807) required *sociètès anonymes* (companies limited by shares) to have "one or more commissioners," shareholders or nonshareholders—whose appointment was *mandatory*—in charge of submitting, before the annual general meeting, a report on the financial situation of the company, its balance sheet, and the accounts drafted by the directors. The report was meant as a prerequisite for the approval of the balance sheet and the accounts during the general meeting. The commissioners had the power to conduct inspections over the company's books as well as the transactions entered into by the company (Article 32 of Law 24th July 1867). Therefore, similar functions were provided under British and French legislation at that time, but the difference was that the appointment of auditors started as a default rule in the United Kingdom, while in France, it had been mandatory since 1867, when government authorization for incorporation was abolished. Both jurisdictions, however, had a one-tier board at that time as both the auditors in the UK and the commissioners in France *were not* an internal body of the company and were merely exercising accounting functions. Later on, other European legislation followed, but their solutions were different: some of them allocated to the body—conceived as an organ of the company, that is, an internal body—also the power to *supervise and judge* directors' activities; others decided—following the UK and French path—to provide for external auditors, in charge of merely *checking* financial statements and other accounts. The former group basically conceived a two-tier board. Germany, however, sticks out since, in addition to supervisory powers, the supervisory board could be (and still is) allocated the power to authorize or decide on the most important strategies and managerial acts. A German law dated 1870 provided for the mandatory appointment of a supervisory board, which is made of three members chosen among the shareholders and is in charge of supervising the directors' conduct of business; collecting information on the company's affairs; examining books, accounts, financial statements, and proposals for the distribution of dividends; and verifying actual cash flow. The body had the duty to report the results before the general meeting each year and had the power to represent the company in legal proceedings against the directors and to convene a general meeting when this was deemed proper for the company's interest (Articles 193, 194, 209, and 225 of German law dated 1870). They were personally liable (Articles 204, 225, ivi) whenever, upon their knowledge, contributions were given back to the shareholders, company shares were bought back, dividends or interests were distributed with no net profits, and the like.

In Italy, when the Commercial Code of 1865 was amended in 1882, a mandatory board of internal (or statutory) auditors (*sindaci*) was introduced; since then, both the board of directors and the board of internal auditors have been appointed in a general meeting of shareholders. The introduction of such an organ resulted in a two-tier *horizontal* board structure in Italian companies and historically represented one of the most significant changes to the 1865 Commercial Code, which was, up to then, entirely based upon the French Code, under which, as above explained, companies limited by shares had a one-tier board structure, with the stockholders at a general meeting electing the board of directors. The board of internal auditors, appointed among the shareholders or nonshareholders in a general meeting, was in charge of the widest power to permanently supervise the company's affairs, registers, accounts, and financial statements and to convene a general meeting whenever this was deemed proper.[15] This was argued to be a system that better responded to the needs of the trade and aligned to the practice already common among big companies in Italy.[16] The main underlying reason for its introduction was to offset the abolition of government authorization for the setting up of companies and its power of control: at that point, the need for an organ that was *independent* from the directors and in charge of wide powers over them was fundamental to protect shareholders' interests without allocating merely to the directors the safeguarding of the company's affairs.[17] It had been clear, since then, that one of the main dangers within companies limited by shares was the difficulty for shareholders to supervise the management of the company for various reasons: the extension and complexity of the business or the location of company's affairs often very far from the company's registered seat or from shareholders. For these reasons, it was decided to insert in the Italian Commercial Code, and taking inspiration from foreign legislation or bills, the election by the general meeting of shareholders of one or more persons (called censors, or commissioners or supervisory board under foreign legislations) in charge of exercising over the company's management "the control and the continuous critical and effective tools" that shareholders, as matter of fact, were not able to exercise.[18] This board was—and currently is[19]—in charge of permanently overseeing companies' compliance with all provisions of law and the articles of association, examining shareholders' complaints, and ensuring the representation of collective interests—upon its own initiative or upon the mandate by the general meeting of stockholders—whenever the directors are in conflict with the shareholders' views and interests. Therefore, the *sindaci* were made a third party, a sort of arbitrator between the directors' and shareholders' interests. This was the rationale behind Article 150 of the Commercial Code, which provided that in case of self-dealing transactions, the directors were required to notify the same to the other directors, and

[15] See Articles 183 and 184 of the Commercial Code 1882.

[16] See Relazione del Ministro di Grazia e Giustizia e dei Culti (Mancini) od Esposizione dei Motivi del Progetto del Codice di Commercio pel Regno d'Italia, cit., p 409. Even though there were objections since then: Vidari (1888), para. 1007; Behrend (1873), pp. 66–70.

[17] Marghieri (1929), p. 486–490. In order to ensure independence, the Commercial Code required that there should be no family ties between the *sindaci* and the directors. Currently, the Civil Code adds to this requirement also the lack of professional and economic ties with both directors and the company itself (see Article 2399 of the Italian Civil Code) in order for the *sindaci* to be independent.

[18] Reference was made to the following countries: France (Law dated July 24, 1867), Northern Germany (Law dated May 24, 1870), Switzerland (a Bill dated 1864), and Belgium (a Bill dated 1868).

[19] The Italian source of company law is the Civil Code dated 1942, as subsequently amended, in particular by the reform introduced by Legislative Decree N. 6 of 17th January 2003.

the *sindaci* and were obliged to abstain from any resolution on them; in such cases, resolutions should have been approved by the *sindaci* themselves. Nowadays, this provision has disappeared from the Civil Code; however, the *sindaci* are still required to preliminarily give their advice on issues like the remuneration of executive directors—which is a typical issue of potential conflict of interests.[20] But no dualism was conceived between the *sindaci* and the directors: they are two forces converging toward the same aim, namely, the best interest of the company. In any case, the *sindaci* are not allowed to interfere with the conduct of the company's business, which duty is allocated to the board of directors solely. Additionally, the role was meant to be permanent; that is why a rule was (and still is) in force under which companies are required to appoint, at the same time, regular and substitute *sindaci*: the latter category replaces the regular *sindaci* if, for any reason, one or more of them should be missing (because of resignation, dismissal, death, etc.).[21] This horizontal two-tier board model was confirmed by the Civil Code, issued in 1942, and was the sole possible model for companies until 2003, when the Reform of company law was passed (see below in Section 6.4.6.1).

In France, the situation changed after the passing of Law N. 66-537 of 24th July 1966. Its main amendment to the previous regulation of companies limited by shares was to provide for the possibility of choosing between the traditional one-tier board and a new model, the two-tier vertical board introduced—following German legislation—to ensure a better distribution and separation of powers between the management body (*le Directoire*), whose independence was strengthened, and a supervisory body (*le Conseil de Surveillance*) whose function was to exercise a permanent control over the management.[22] The introduction of the two-tier vertical board model was also originally meant to strengthen the role of employee representatives within the board, taking inspiration from the German model of companies, but this proposal was eventually rejected by the Senate. In this respect, the one-tier and two-tier board models in France do not differ from each other: in both cases, employee representatives can be granted—if companies so decide in articles of association—advisory powers in the supervisory board (in the two-tier model) or in the board of directors (in the one-tier model).[23] However, since French Law N. 504/2013, companies with over 5000 employees (in France) or over 10,000 (internationally) are obliged to appoint employee representatives. It is upon the supervisory body to appoint the members of the management body and its chairman; it is strictly forbidden for members to sit in both bodies at the same time, but it is allowed for a member of the supervisory body who resigns to be appointed as a member of the management body. At the same time, the role of the *commissaires aux comptes* was reinforced and made more effective by ensuring stricter independence

[20] See Article 2389, subsection 3, of the Italian Civil Code.

[21] See Article 2401 of the Italian Civil Code.

[22] Ripert and Roblot (2002), p. 239.

[23] Ripert and Roblot (2002), pp. 470–471.

requirements.[24] The default rule is that the management body is allocated the widest power to act on behalf of the company by taking decisions necessary to carry out business activity as identified in the object clause. However, the articles of association may limit such powers by conditioning its exercise upon prior authorization by the supervisory body. In case the supervisory body refuses its authorization, the management body can carry out the activity only if the general meeting of shareholders resolves to vote in favor of it.[25] Members of the supervisory body are appointed in the general meeting of shareholders; the law does not require that those members meet special professional qualifications.

Nowadays, among the main listed companies, companies with a two-tier board represent a strong minority, roughly 20%, while roughly 80% have opted for the one-tier board.[26] In the past, many companies used to adopt the two-tier board model but now switched to the one-tier board system. Often, those companies that have chosen the two-tier model show strong family ownership.[27]

In Germany, the current legislation on public companies limited by shares is the *Aktiengesellschaft*, enacted in 1965 (and amended since then). Public companies must adopt a two-tier board where the shareholders, at a general meeting, appoint the board of directors (*Vorstand*), which, in turn, appoints the supervisory board (*Aufsichtsrat*), which is vested with supervisory powers as well as strategic decision-making and directing powers over the *Vorstand*. The *Aufsichtsrat* shall be composed of at least three members. Further to various statutes enacted since the 1950s, most important companies are characterized by having within *Aufsichtsrat* as members some employees' representatives appointed by employees; this system is called *Mitbestimmung*. According to *Mitbtestimmung* rule, companies in coal and steel industries must have half members of the *Aufsichtsrat* appointed by shareholders and half appointed by employees and the chair shall be appointed by both parties (under the Coal and Steel Codetermination Act dated 1951). Since 1976, pursuant to the Codetermination Act, this system has been extended to all companies, regardless of industry, but with different rules: (i) in companies with over 2000 employees, half of the members of the *Aufsichtsrat* are appointed by the employees and half by the shareholders, but the chair, in the absence of an agreement, is appointed by the shareholders, while the employees appoint the vice chair, and (ii) in companies with over 500 employees, employees have the right to appoint merely 1/3 of the members of the *Aufsichtsrat*, and these members are designated with a consultancy role only and have no decision power within the board (under the One-Third Participation Act dated 2004). However, in practice, many companies voluntarily appoint employee representatives in the *Aufsichtsrat*, even if not legally

[24] Ripert and Roblot (2002), p. 239.

[25] Ripert and Roblot (2002), pp. 457–460.

[26] See www.kramerlevin.com/a/web/48943/190222-The-Legal-500-Reid-Feldman-France-Corporate-Governance.pdf.

[27] For examples of French companies with two-tier boards, see Europcar, Hermes International, Michelin, Peugeot, Vivendi, etc.

required, in order to facilitate relationships with the workforce. Also, other jurisdictions, such as the Nordic countries and the Netherlands, provide for similar systems of *Mitbestimmung*.

Therefore, we can conclude that, nowadays, it is possible to envisage in Europe one-tier, two-tier, and hybrid board models; some jurisdictions have as board members employee representatives. Comparing the US and UK jurisdictions (which offer a one-tier board model) on one side and European jurisdictions on the other side, we can say that there is actually a European identity with reference to board models, in that different variations of the two-tier board models are widely used in various continental European countries in addition to the one-tier board model, which is less commonly adopted.[28]

6.4 Italian Companies: Sources of Law

Even though European company law is largely harmonized with reference to public companies, differences remain across jurisdictions. It would be impossible to cover the company law of all member states in this book. Therefore, reference will be made to only one of the member states, Italy, to then compare Italian law with other European jurisdictions (mainly French and German law) with reference to the most important issues and when there are some peculiarities distinguishing Italian from other jurisdictions.

Since Italy belongs to the European Union, at the apex of its sources of law is European Union law, as explained above. Other sources are:

1. Civil Code 1942, amended many times and most importantly, for companies, in 2004 (Reform of company law)
2. Legislative Decree N. 58/1998, as amended, regulating listed companies
3. Consob (the Italian Stock Exchange Authority) Regulations with reference to listed companies and the financial market
4. Case law/legal doctrine

In addition, for listed companies, it has to be mentioned the Corporate Governance Code (latest edition is 2020), which is not a hard source of law since it is subject to the "comply or explain" rule: it is rather a soft source of law, that is, a set of best practice recommendations with reference to corporate governance, which companies are encouraged to follow in order to attract investments from the market.

[28]To expand on the Nordic countries that show various hybrid models: Hanse and Lonfeldt (2014), pp. 124–128.

6.4.1 Ownership Pattern in Italian-Listed Companies

The Italian financial market can be classified as an insider system (see Section 4.2 above). The control of listed companies is mainly exercised by families, the state, or a few strategic shareholders often linked among themselves by voting agreements, whereby uniform decisions are taken. These agreements may also find implementation through exchanges of share ownership (circular or cross-shareholdings). The reasons for such a structure are to be found in the evolution of Italian economic history: the productive structure of the country has entrepreneurs who run the business, centralizing all decisions, which is a typical feature not only for small and medium firms but also for larger firms. However, since the beginning of the twentieth century, in order to counterbalance the high concentration of ownership in the private sector, the state entrepreneur intervened to finance companies and, in many cases, to actually take over businesses in situations of crisis. In later times, however, the law encouraged greater dispersion of public shareholding also through institutional investors; the growing competition within the globalized markets and within the European Union requires greater access to capital resources for companies, whereas traditional sources of capital (the banking system or government investment spending) do not seem to be sufficient or viable any longer to fulfill the needs of the economic system at large. The offer of shares of companies owned by the state to the public started under Law No. 474/1994, regulating the procedure for the privatization of state-owned companies; since then, major banks, the biggest Italian insurance company, the giant gas and energy company Eni s.p.a., the telecommunications company Telecom Italia (nowadays TIM), and others have been privatized.

As of the end of 2023, the figures confirm the small size of Italian equity securities markets when compared to other European exchanges as companies listed on the main stock exchange (Euronext Milan (EXM)) were 210. While the average stake held by the largest shareholder is equal to 49.1%, the average stake held by the market is equal to 38.3%. In more detail, the ownership structure is as follows.

Ownership Structure of Italian-Listed Companies (as Average)

Core shareholders (blockholders) = 49.1% (family members who are major core shareholders = 62.4% of those companies; state and local entities who are core shareholders = 11.9%)

Financial institutions = 2.4%

Mixed = 4.8%

No ultimate controlling agent (UCA) = 18.6%[29]

[29] See Consob (2023), pp. 12–20.

6.4.2 How to Set Up a Company: Types of Companies

The fundamental characteristic of companies is set forth in Article 2325, paragraph 1, of the Civil Code for public companies and in Article 2462, paragraph 1, for private companies, which establish the limited liability of members with regard to a company's obligations. The articles state:

> A company's liability for its obligations is limited to its assets.

From these articles, one can deduce that members and also those who represent the company are not personally liable for the company's obligations. This is the basic principle that differentiates companies from partnerships. As was mentioned above (Section 3.3), in some cases, partners can enjoy limited liability with respect to a partnership's liabilities (for example, limited partners or partners in a noncommercial partnership), but in no case is it possible for managing partners to limit their liability. By contrast, in companies, neither the members nor the directors are personally liable for a company's obligations. Creditors can only enforce their claims against the company's own assets. For this latter reason, a fundamental part of the rules governing companies deals with safeguarding a company's share capital in that the latter constitutes the most important form of security for third parties entertaining legal relations with the company.

There are three types of companies:

1. Public companies limited by shares (with share capital) (*società per azioni, s.p.a.*)
2. Private companies (with capital divided into quotas; there are no shares) (*società a responsabilità limitata, s.r.l.*)
3. limited partnership-company (with share capital, where some members enjoy limited liability, while others do not, *società in accomandita per azioni, s.a.p.a.*)

All companies are entities with their own legal personality, separate and distinct from that of their members; they acquire rights and obligations in their own name and enjoy full legal capacity. They come into being upon registration with the Registry of Enterprises. For each type of company, a minimum capital to be subscribed by the members has been established by the Civil Code (in addition to the Second European Union Directive). For public companies, the minimum capital is €50,000; for private companies, it is €10,000 (unless it is a "simplified private company" (*s.r.l. semplificata*), in which case the symbolic amount is €1 euro; the latter type has been thought for start-up companies and is subject to special requirements, in particular with reference to its object, which must be innovative, as specified by a decree issued by the Minister of Justice); for a limited partnership-company, the minimum capital is €50.000.

Companies must be formed by a public deed drawn up by a notary. The two basic incorporation documents are:

1. The articles of association and
2. The bylaws

The articles of association must indicate the name of the shareholders, the name of the company, the corporate object, the share capital, and all other matters set forth in Article 2328 of the Civil Code (and in Article 2463 for private companies). The bylaws contain the company's internal regulations and must be attached to the memorandum of association. After having drawn up the memorandum and articles of association, the notary files them with the Registry of Enterprises (of the area where the company has its registered office), which checks compliance with the legal formalities for forming a company and directs that the company be enrolled in the Registry of Enterprises, whereby the company acquires legal personality with effect from registration.

Public and private companies can be formed by one or more members, while limited partnership-company must have at least two shareholders.

As mentioned, the capital of a public company is represented by shares. Whoever subscribes or otherwise acquires a share becomes a shareholder. The value of all the capital contributions made by the shareholders must be equal to at least the share capital subscribed. Since the share capital is divided into shares, the figure for share capital divided by the number of shares issued gives us the nominal value of each share. However, based on the Reform dated 2003, shares may not have a nominal value; it has to be specified in the articles of association. In case shares have a nominal value, Article 2346 of the Civil Code provides that shares may not be issued for sums lower than their nominal value. What this means is that shares cannot be issued if the subscriber therefore does not pay or undertake to pay a sum of money at least equal to the nominal value of the number of shares to be allotted to him.

Example on Incorporation

Mr. X and Y set up a public company, "Z," with a share capital equal to €200,000. X subscribes to buy shares for €100,000, and Y subscribes for €100,000. The share capital is divided into 100 shares: each share therefore has a nominal value of €2000. Both X and Y can subscribe to 50 shares each by paying or undertaking to pay €100,000 each. The 50 shares issued to X and the other 50 shares issued to Z must have a nominal value of €2000 each and, thus, an overall value of €100,000 for X and €100,000 for Y.

With reference to public companies, members must:

1. Fully subscribe to the share capital (either in cash or in kind within the limits provided for in Articles 2254 and 2255 Civil Code), and
2. Deposit at least three-tenths of the cash contributions with a credit institution

Shares are freely transferable, meaning the identity of the holder thereof is of no relevance.

6.4.3 Private Companies and Limited Partnership-Companies

The regulation of private companies (*s.r.l.*) can be found in Article 2462 and subsequent provisions of the Civil Code. As above mentioned, Italian private companies have no shares: their capital is divided into quotas. The consequence is that in order to transfer quotas, more formalities are required compared to shares, and the intervention of a notary or a qualified accountant is needed. Another difference concerns internal organization. Only the traditional board model is provided for private companies under the Civil Code, and therefore, alternative board models cannot be adopted (see Section 6.4.4). In addition, there is more flexibility concerning internal organization in private companies compared to public companies, if we consider that a general meeting of shareholders is not mandatory for the adoption of resolutions: the Civil Code provides for the possibility of adopting written resolutions if so provided in the articles of association.

With reference to limited partnerships-companies (*s.a.p.a.*), regulation is provided under Article 2452 and subsequent articles of the Civil Code. The most peculiar feature is the distinction between limited (*soci accomandanti*) and unlimited (*soci accomandatari*) shareholders: following the same pattern already analyzed for partnerships (see Section 3.3.4), the first category of shareholders shall be liable for the company's obligations only up to the contributions made when subscribing to the shares of the company and has no managerial or representation power in the company, while the latter category can be appointed as directors and is also personally liable for the company's obligations. Capital is divided into shares. Also, *s.a.p.a.*, like public companies, may choose to adopt any of the three board models (see Section 6.4.4), which must be indicated in the articles of association; otherwise, the default model would be the traditional one. All other articles on public companies under the Civil Code shall apply to *s.a.p.a.*, as specified thereunder.

6.4.4 Public Companies: Models of Boards of Directors

The Italian Civil Code, further to the Reform dated 2003 and the consequential amendments-, provides for the possibility for shareholders of a public company to choose among *three board models* (Article 2380 Civil Code). The model chosen shall be mentioned in the articles of association. If the articles of association are silent on this issue, the so-called traditional board model shall apply; in other words, the default model is the traditional one.

Basically, with the reform of company law, the Italian legislature has chosen not to impose a model. What have been the reasons for providing three different models of governance rather than just one, as had been originally stated since the Commercial Code dated 1882 and confirmed by the Civil Code in 1942 (see above Section 6.3)? One justification was to make the Italian system more similar to other jurisdictions that recognize one-tier and two-tier vertical board models, as seen above. Also, efficiency justifications have been highlighted by the Reform of 2003: leaving companies with the freedom of choice would allow them to adapt the governance model to particular needs. In this respect, it has to be clarified that international empirical research—mainly devoting its interest to comparing the one-tier UK board vs. the German two-tier vertical board—does not show any conclusive evidence of the superiority of one model over the other. Both systems may offer effective corporate governance, and it is not possible to assign superiority to either of them.[30] We will consider that corporate governance rules are efficient if they solve agency problems (between controlling and minority shareholders/ executives and shareholders) and if they balance powers within the company according to the ownership structure of each financial system. Therefore, there is no board model that *per se* may ensure effective corporate governance; board models are not like labels that can be used to ensure efficiency, also because specific rules for each board model may differ from one jurisdiction to another. In this respect, it is worth pointing out the OECD *Principles on Corporate Governance* (based on empirical studies and fundamental economic research), according to which efficiency depends on the specific set of rules, for each model in an organization, on the distribution of powers and duties, qualification, effectiveness, independence, enforcement/legal instruments, and accountability; meanwhile, no board model worldwide has proven to be "the best."[31] By contrast, some academics argued the superiority of the one-tier board, pointing out the flow of information theory, which states that the allocation of both supervisory and strategic powers —which are complementary to one another—to a single board makes those in charge of control work more effectively, while in the two-tier board, access to information by members of the supervisory organ is more limited.[32] In the two-tier model, the flow of information from the management to the supervisory board and within the latter from the chairman to the other members can be very weak, especially if members are too many and do not frequently meet.[33] At the same time, it was argued that in the two-tier model, the function of the supervisory board is not merely the exercise of controlling powers over the management but, historically, also that of building networking relationships with stakeholders: from this viewpoint, the supposed superiority of the one-tier model cannot be advocated.[34] (In this respect, if we compare the Italian traditional model (i.e., the two-tier horizontal model) with the two-tier vertical model, the flow of information theory cannot apply because

[30] Jungmann (2006), pp. 426–474.

[31] OECD (2003), p. 18.

[32] Davies (2001), pp. 15–20.

[33] Hopt (1998), pp. 241–245.

[34] Davies (2001).

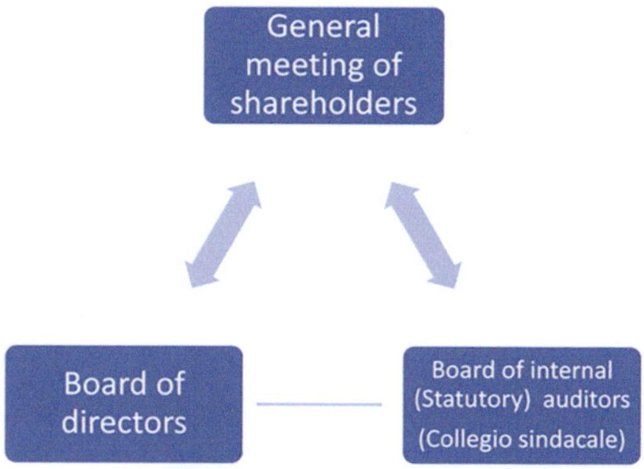

Fig. 6.1 The two-tier horizontal (traditional) model. Source: Author's own elaboration

Fig. 6.2 The two-tier vertical model. Source: Author's own elaboration

Fig. 6.3 The one-tier model. Source: Author's own elaboration

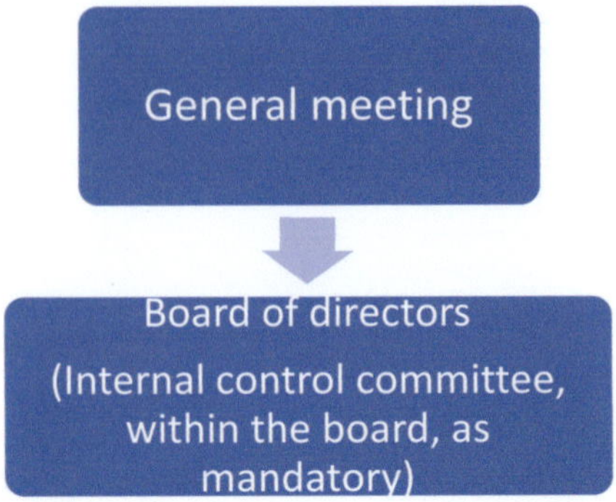

members of the board of internal auditors are personally obliged, under the Civil Code, to attend all board and executive committee meetings, having therefore immediate access to all information similar to the directors in the one-tier board.)

Having specified these general aspects, we are going to examine Italian core rules on board models, also in the context of evaluating how sound Italian corporate governance is.

In the two-tier horizontal (traditional) model, both the board of directors and the board of internal (statutory) auditors are appointed in the general meeting of shareholders. See Fig. 6.1.

In the two-tier vertical (dualistic) model, the shareholders at a general meeting appoint the supervisory board, which, in turn, appoints the management board; see Fig. 6.2.

In the one-tier (monistic) model, the general meeting of shareholders appoints the board of directors, some members of which *must* compose the internal control committee; see Fig. 6.3.

6.4.5 Public Companies: Allocation of Powers Between the General Meeting of Shareholders and the Board of Directors

The Italian Civil Code provides mainly for mandatory rules in allocating powers within a company, which depends on the board model chosen by the company. Within such a statutory framework, the powers of the general meeting of shareholders are then determined. The articles of association are granted a few possibilities to arrange their own rules on the allocation of powers, apart from the fundamental choice of the board model.

While the management of the company belongs to the board of directors in all three models, there are differences with reference to the general meeting of shareholders. If the model adopted is the *one-tier* and *two-tier horizontal models*, the main powers of the ordinary general meeting are:

1. Approval of financial statements and distribution of dividends
2. Appointment/dismissal/liability of directors, internal auditors, and external auditors
3. Remuneration of directors, internal auditors, and external auditors
4. Authorization for the directors' acts, if so provided under the articles of association

If the model adopted is the *two-tier vertical model*, the main powers of the ordinary general meeting of shareholders are:

1. Appointment/dismissal/remuneration/liability of the members of the supervisory board
2. Appointment/dismissal/remuneration/liability of external auditors
3. Distribution of dividends

No approval of financial statements by the general meeting of shareholders is provided in the *two-tier vertical model* unless the supervisory board does not approve them or when 1/3 of the board of directors require shareholders' vote, if the articles of association so provide.

If companies are *listed*, the general meeting of shareholders is additionally allocated the following powers in *all board models*:

1. Approval of defensive measures in the case of hostile takeovers
2. Approval of stock-option plans for directors, managers, and top employees
3. Delisting of the company
4. Authorization to increase cross-holdings over 2%
5. Approval of directors' remuneration report (policy)

Powers allocated to the *extraordinary general meeting* of shareholders are the same for all board models:

1. Amendments to the articles of association and bylaws (including the issuance of new shares, mergers, and split-offs)
2. Appointment of liquidators and fixing of their powers

In all board models, the general meeting expresses the will of the company's members, and voting is on a majority basis. The meeting can be either ordinary or extraordinary. Differences relate to the matters to be resolved (see the above list), the thresholds required to approve a resolution (higher for extraordinary meetings since issues are more fundamental), and the formalities for drawing up the minutes of the meeting (a notary must draw up those of an extraordinary general meeting). However, in order to convene both meetings all the formalities provided under Article 2366 and subsequent provisions of the Civil Code shall be complied with.

The resolutions of both ordinary and extraordinary general meetings may be challenged before the courts of the place in which the company has its registered office in two cases:

1. If the resolutions do not comply with law or the articles of association, or
2. If the object of the resolutions is illegal or impossible or there are no minutes or no meeting was convened

In the former case, it is a question of voidability (*annullabilità*), whereas in the latter case, it is a question of voidness (*nullità*), pure and simple. Voidable resolutions may be challenged by absent or dissenting members (reaching certain thresholds), the directors, or statutory auditors within 3 months from the date of the adoption of the resolution or within 3 months from the date of registration of the resolution if it is one subject to registration in the Registry of Enterprises. Void resolutions may be challenged by any interested party within 3 years (the starting date is the same as for voidable resolutions).

6.4.6 Public Companies: The Board of Directors in the Three Models: Qualification and Independence

The management of a company is entrusted to a board of directors, in all models, which may exercise its management powers with maximum independence. The power to represent the company is vested in one or more directors, and such directors may perform all acts falling within the ambit of the company's object. However, Article 2384 of the Civil Code provides that any limitations on the powers of representation of the directors cannot be enforced against third parties, who may rely on those representation powers belonging to all directors; likewise, acts that are outside of the company's object are *binding* on the company *vis-à-vis* third parties despite the fact that, in both cases, the restrictions in question are published in the company's memorandum and articles of association or other documents filed with the Registry of Enterprises. This rule, which is typical of companies (and different from partnerships; see Chap. 3 above), applies to all European companies as it has been introduced by the First EC Directive, with the aim of safeguarding the rights of third parties and their reliance on the validity of contracts and other acts entered into by the directors on behalf of the company, even if there are irregularities. There is a theoretical rationale justifying this rule, that is, that directors are conceived as organs of the company, and through them, the company as a legal person may act; this is why this kind of representation is called "organic representation." Through directors, companies enjoy full legal capacity, same as individuals, and no limits to their representation powers can be inferred by the company's object. While in partnerships (under all jurisdictions; see Sections 3.2.5, 3.3, 3.4.1 above), the object of the activity sets the boundaries of members' agency powers, in companies this is not the case: a company is a legal person enjoying full legal capacity and may act (entering into contracts or even committing torts) through its organs, i.e. directors.

However, the Civil Code also provides that if a company proves that a third party intentionally acted to damage the company, that is, not only knowing the directors lacked representative powers but also acting in bad faith and with fraudulent intent to cause damage to the company, the acts carried out by one or more directors do not bind the company.

Directors may or may not be members of the company.

Provisions for directors are basically the same in the three models, with a few exceptions. With reference to *qualifications*, there is no compulsory qualification for directors. Voluntarily, according to Article 2387 of the Civil Code, the articles of association may provide for professionality, independence, or honorability requirements. For listed companies, however, under Legislative Decree N. 58/1998, honorability requirements are mandatory, meaning no conviction for any crime specified by legislation. In addition, for listed companies, the Corporate Governance Code can be mentioned, which recommends that "All directors ensure professional skills and competence that are appropriate to their tasks" (Article 2, Principle V).

With reference to *effectiveness*, only for listed companies in all models, Legislative Decree N. 58/1998 provides for limits to cumulative functions (fixed under the Consob Regulation) (Article 148-*bis*). Similarly, the Corporate Governance Code recommends members of managing and supervisory boards to devote all necessary time to carry out their functions (Article 3, Principle XII).

With reference to *independence*, there are some differences among the three models. Under the traditional model, independence is voluntary and to be decided in the articles of association (Article 2387 of the Civil Code). However, for listed companies, pursuant to Legislative Decree N. 58/1998, Article 147-*ter*, at least one member must comply with the independence requirement; if there are more than seven members, at least two members shall meet the independence requirements. In the two-tier board model, the provision for nonlisted companies is the same, i.e., no mandatory independence requirement. However, for listed companies, under Legislative decree N. 58/1998 (Article 147-*quater*), if members are more than four, at least one shall meet the independence requirements. If the company adopts the one-tier board model, under the Civil Code (Article 2409-*septiesdecies*), at least 1/3 of the members shall be independent (those members will make up the internal supervisory committee); the same 1/3 rule applies to listed companies.

The *definition of independence* for directors of listed companies is the same for all models and is established by Legislative Decree N. 58/1998, Article 148 c. 3. There shall be:

1. no family ties with other directors (also those belonging to the same group of companies);
2. no employment, commercial, business or professional relationships with the company or its directors (including other companies belonging to the same group).

As can be noted, no reference is made to the controlling shareholder/s in terms of assessment of independence despite the fact that Italy is classified as an insider financial system with concentrated ownership. However, in this respect, the Corporate Governance Code expands the notion, mentioning, among the circumstances *that jeopardize or appear to jeopardize independence*, also:

> Being a significant shareholder of the company or an executive director or employee of the company or of a significant shareholder of the company (during the previous 3 years); holding significant commercial, financial or professional relationship with the company, its executives, and those who control the company (during the previous 3 years) (Article 2, Recommendation 7).

The Corporate Governance Code devotes also other provisions to independence, stating that a "*significant number* of non-executive directors is independent" (Article 2, Principle VI) and, more precisely, that:

> At least two other than the Chair"; for "large companies with concentrated ownership at least 1/3"; for "other large companies at least half" (Article 2, Recommendation 5).

Under the Corporate Governance Code, it is upon the board of directors to assess the independence of members each year. Other circumstances that jeopardize or appear to jeopardize independence therein mentioned are:

> Significant remuneration from the company (during the previous 3 years); being member of the board for more than 9 years; holding cross directorship; being external auditor of the company; being close relative of a person who is in any of the positions mentioned above.

However, it is up to the board of directors to define *ex ante* such criteria in detail (Article 2, Recommendation 5).

The Corporate Governance Code assigns to independent directors, as a main task, to be members of the *internal committees* that listed companies are recommended to establish within the board of directors in the three models. The internal committees are allocated "preliminary, propositional and consultative functions" on hot issues, that is, those issues that may involve conflicts of interest for executive directors. These issues are remuneration, risk and internal control, and nomination. The recommendation by the Corporate Governance Code is that internal committees (i.e., remuneration committee, risk and internal control committee, and nomination committee) should be made up of nonexecutive directors, a majority of whom at least are *independent*, to support the board (see Article 3, Recommendation 16; Article 4, Recommendation 20; Article 5, Recommendation 26; Article 6, Recommendation 26—each recommendation referring to each internal committee).

6.4.6.1 The Board of Directors in the Three Models: Composition in Listed Companies

One of the most peculiar characteristics of Italian company law, with reference to listed companies, is the right of minority shareholders to appoint one or more members of the board of directors, so-called *minority directors*. From a law and economic perspective, this rule has been introduced to face the agency problem, typical of concentrated financial systems, between controlling and minority shareholders. Minority directors would check and balance the power of directors appointed by controlling shareholders by preventing any possible opportunistic behavior, which could consist in pursuing the interests of the latter to the detriment of the minority shareholders or the company itself. Under the law (Civil Code), all directors must act in the interest of the company, as shall be seen below (Section 6.4.6.2). But the directors appointed by the controlling shareholders might be induced, as a matter of fact and in breach of the Civil Code provisions, to enhance the interests of the latter rather than the company's interest. Thus, the appointment of "minority directors" is thought to protect the company itself and the minority shareholders from any potential opportunistic behavior, which could occur in practice despite being prohibited under the law. In other words, it is a legal device to balance controlling shareholders' power, which should make the board more independent from blockholders. Minority directors were introduced by the Law on Privatization N. 474/1994 in order to enhance the participation of foreign institutional investors in Italian-listed companies.[35]

Therefore, under Article 147-*ter*, subsection 3, of Legislative Decree N. 58/1998, minority shareholders are granted appointment rights through the following mechanism: one or more shareholders reaching a threshold not higher than 1/40 of the share capital (the threshold is fixed in the articles of association and regulated by Article 144-*quater* of Consob Regulations N. 11971/1999, specifying share between the range of 0.5% and 4.5% of the share capital, depending on the company's capitalization) shall prepare their own list of candidates. In addition to the directors appointed by the majority, at least one director must be a candidate, obtaining the most votes, among the list/s presented by the minority, provided that she/he is not linked, in any way (even indirectly), to the list that won the elections.

Comparing the Italian rule with the proposed SEC Shareholder Access Rule (Rule 14a-11) under US law (see Section 4.3.9.3), one can notice the sharp difference: the SEC-proposed Rule would have allowed minority shareholders just to nominate one or more candidates with no guarantee of her/his election by the general meeting of shareholders, whereas, in Italy, minority shareholders, as explained, have the right to appoint (not just nominate) one or more directors.

With reference to minority directors, there are, however, some differences among the three models. Under the traditional model, at least one director must be appointed by the minority shareholders, and there are no prerequisites (see Article 147-*ter*,

[35] Other European member states provide for similar rules to enhance minority shareholders' rights, such as Austria, Greece, Denmark, Finland, the Netherlands, and Portugal.

subsection 3, Legislative Decree N. 58/1998). Under the two-tier board model, there is no such rule for members of the board of directors simply because, as explained under Section 6.4.4, the shareholders do not appoint the directors. Under the one-tier board model, at least one director must be appointed by the minority shareholders, but honorability, professionality, and independence prerequisites are provided for minority directors (see Article 147-*ter*, subsection 3, Legislative Decree N. 58/1998).

Another requirement stated under Italian law with reference to listed companies and composition refers to gender diversity. Pursuant to Article 147-*ter*, subsection 1-*ter*, of Legislative Decree N. 58/1998, lately amended in 2019, at least 2/5 of the board's seats shall be reserved to the least represented gender. The provision was originally introduced in 2011 and was justified by the consistent discrimination against potential female board members in companies, reflecting the broader discrimination and gap existing in society. Before 2011, female directors in Italian-listed companies were only 6% of the members, one of the worst numbers among the European member states. The requirement began from elections of board members in 2012 and should have been in force for only six mandates (each mandate lasting for 3 years): in other words, it was conceived not as a permanent rule but as a so-called sunset clause. The underlying reason for not being a permanent rule was that time and culture should balance the gender gap in reaching top positions in listed companies. However, since the European Parliament has adopted the abovementioned Directive N. 2022/2381/UE, requiring the same mandatory composition (see Section 6.2 above), it shall be assumed that the Italian time limit will disappear when the European Directive will be implemented in Italy. The gender requirement under the same Article 147-*ter* of Legislative Decree N.58/1998 is assisted by a sanction by Consob (the Italian stock market authority), which has both the power to fine a company that does not comply with the rule and the power to order compliance; if the breach persists, Consob has the power to eventually dissolve the board. Apart from social and economic considerations, briefly summarized above, diversity in board composition is also thought to improve corporate governance. It was highlighted, for instance, that "Diversity of expertise and viewpoints among members of supervisory and management boards may favor a good understanding of the company's organization and its activities. It allows members to challenge decisions proposed by executives and to be more open to innovation and new ideas, halting in this way group thinking among members. . .," while the lack of diverse opinions, values, and expertise results in the "absence of debate, shortage of ideas and critical sense within boards" and may also produce "a negative impact on supervision and balance of powers of boards of directors."[36]

[36] See European Directive N. 2014/95/UE, Whereas N. 18; Commission Staff Working Document Executive Summary of the Impact Assessment Accompanying the Document Proposal for a Directive of the European Parliament and of the Council amending Council Directives 78/660/EEC and 83/349/EEC as regards disclosure of non-financial and diversity information by certain large companies and groups /* SWD/2013/0128 final. The latter document also highlights that there is no market incentive that fosters, by itself, enterprises to change the current situation (with the

Apart from gender diversity, no other diversity in composition of boards is required under Italian legislation. However, the Corporate Governance Code recommends listed companies:

> to apply diversity criteria, including gender ones, to the composition of the board of directors, ensuring the primary objective of adequate competence and professionalism of its members (see Principle 2, Recommendation VII).

Therefore, according to the Corporate Governance Code, the choice of what diversity criteria shall be considered by companies is left to the board of directors. There is no specific reference; rather, it is highlighted that the primary focus should be merit and no other criterion.

6.4.6.2 Public Companies: Directors' Duties and Liabilities

Directors are obliged to comply with the duties imposed on them by law and by the memorandum and articles of association and to manage the company with care, to be evaluated according to a double test under Article 2392 of the Civil Code: subjective (that is, considering the specific expertise a director may have) and objective (that is, applying the criterion of reasonableness, which any director must meet). It has to be noted that the double test, introduced in Italy with the Reform dated 2003, took inspiration from the provision contained under the UK Companies Act (see Section 5.7 above).

If the directors fail to perform their duties properly, thereby causing *damage to the company*, they can be sued by the company itself for breach of directors' duties, subject to a resolution adopted in an ordinary general meeting of shareholders, which is considered passed if the majority shareholders consent, or by the supervisory boards, in the case of traditional and two-tier vertical models (Articles 2393 and 2409-*decies* of the Civil Code). Alternatively, minority shareholders reaching 1/5 or 1/40 of the share capital or a lower threshold fixed in the bylaws may bring a *derivative action* on behalf of the company (Article 2393-*bis* of the Civil Code). In this case, it being a derivative action for the damage suffered by the company, if the directors are held liable, they shall pay damages to the company itself. Who is going to bear the legal costs for the suit? Under Article 2393-*bis* of the Civil Code, the company shall reimburse the legal costs to the plaintiffs in the derivative action "just in case of success in the proceeding," that is, only if the directors are held liable by the court. In other words, the risk to pay expenses for filing an action is borne by the minority shareholders: if their claim is rejected by the courts, they shall pay for the legal costs. This rule is certainly not an incentive to bring derivative actions.

Furthermore, directors who breach the duties provided under the Civil Code for the preservation of the integrity of the share capital may be held liable by the

---

female gender being the least represented in Europe), even though there are asymmetries among member states, and this is another reason that makes a legislative mandatory intervention necessary.

company's *creditors*, who may start a legal action if the company's assets are insufficient to satisfy their claims (Article 2394 of the Civil Code).

Finally, if directors act intentionally or negligently in a way that damages individual shareholders or third parties causing *direct damages* (i.e. which are not the effect of the damage suffered by the company's assets) they may be sued by these parties (Article 2395 of the Civil Code).

With reference to individual shareholders, how can they distinguish if the proper judicial remedy is a derivative action (Article 2393-*bis* of the Civil Code) or a direct action (Article 2395 of the Civil Code)? Let us take some examples.

Examples

Directors mismanage the company and make wrong decisions that cause a reduction in the company's assets; in this case, the proper remedy is a legal suit started by the majority shareholders voting upon it in a general meeting or a derivative action if there is no majority but individual shareholders reach the threshold of 1/5 or 1/40 mentioned above. The applicable provisions are Articles 2393 and 2393-*bis*.

The directors publish financial statements or reports containing misleading information and are (or should be) aware that the information is untrue. One or more shareholders decide to buy additional shares of the company, ignoring the fact that the information is untrue, and suffer direct damage because they paid a price for those shares that is higher than their real value since also the market ignores whether the information is true or not. More precisely, damage will occur when, at any time after the purchase of the shares, the market realizes that those pieces of information were not correct, and the share price drops. The damage suffered by those (and only those) shareholders (or other third parties) will be equal to the balance between the price paid to buy the shares and the subsequent lower share price on the market following the knowledge that information was misleading. The proper Article is 2395.

Therefore, we can sum up the discussion by saying that directors who breach the duties provided under the Civil Code may be held liable to:

1. The company
2. The creditors
3. Individual shareholders or third parties

The identification of the legitimate plaintiff depends on who suffers specific damage.

The Civil Code provides for specific regulation with regard to *directors' interests in transactions*. Pursuant to Article 2391 of the Civil Code, in the case of self-dealing transactions, that is, any transaction that has to be approved by the board of directors and for which one or more directors have a direct or indirect (on behalf of third parties) interest, the involved director/s must disclose such interest to the other members of the board as well as to the supervisory boards, specifying the nature, terms, and other characteristics of their interest. The director/s involved, after disclosure, may join the meeting and vote (i.e., shall not abstain); the board of directors may resolve to enter into the transaction, provided it justifies the company's convenience to enter into it under those circumstances. No shareholders' or other organs' approval is required. The board resolution may be challenged in case of breach of the procedure, as explained, and the director/s may be held liable to the company for any damage suffered by the company itself.

However, if the company is listed, the procedure is more complex and stricter and is regulated, pursuant to Article 2391-*bis* of the Civil Code, by Consob Resolution N. 17221/2010 (as amended by European Directive N. 2017/828). The director/s involved must abstain from voting in the board of directors convened to approve the transaction. In addition, *related party transactions* (that is, those transactions in which the parties are the company, subsidiaries or other companies belonging to the same group, directors, and other top managers directly or indirectly) are classified into two types: minor and major transactions, depending on their economic value, which is proportional to the company's capitalization (such value is fixed by Consob). For minor transactions, there is no other requirement apart from disclosure to the board of directors and supervisory boards. Major transactions instead must be approved by the *independent directors solely* (i.e., they are not approved by the board of directors), and their approval is binding. If the independent directors refuse to approve a transaction, the board may decide (*if the bylaws so provide*) to bring the decision on that transaction before the general meeting of shareholders. If a majority of the minority shareholders at the general meeting approve the transaction, it may be entered into by the company. This mechanism conferring such power to the minority shareholders to hamper any conflict coming from controlling shareholders and those linked to them that do not count in adopting the resolution is called the "white-wash" mechanism or MOM (majority of minority approval). This is another rule conceived to protect the minority shareholders and prevent opportunistic behavior by the controlling shareholders.

6.4.6.3 To Whom Are the Directors' Duties Owed? Italy, Germany, and France: A Comparison

The duties identified by the Civil Code and mentioned above are owed by the directors to the company, which is to be considered shareholders as a whole. There is no consideration of other stakeholders under the Italian Civil Code apart from the creditors, so the duty is owed to them by the directors to preserve the integrity of the share capital, and as above explained, creditors can enforce such a duty only in case the assets of the company are not sufficient to satisfy their claims. In so far as the integrity of the share capital is preserved, directors are obliged under the Civil Code to consider the shareholders' interest. We can therefore say that the Italian Civil Code has adopted the so-called shareholder value approach.

However, because of the European Corporate Sustainability Reporting Directive N. 2022/2464/UE, a new approach emerges for those companies subject to the

Directive (See section 6.2), and the directors shall take into consideration, while managing the company, *also* the positive and negative impacts related to the ESG factors, with a particular focus on contrasting climate change and complying with the Paris Agreement and other climate targets set by the European Union. In any case, European legislation does not supersede the Civil Code provisions, and at the moment, consideration of shareholders' interests is still paramount.

Moreover, with reference to listed companies solely, the Italian Corporate Governance Code recommends the board of directors to lead the company by "pursuing its sustainable success," defined, under Article 1, Principle 1 and Definitions, as:

> the objective that guides the actions of the board of directors and that consists of creating long-term value for the benefit of the shareholders, taking into account the interests of other stakeholders relevant to the company.

In other words, the Corporate Governance Code is fully coherent with the Civil Code (and it could not be any different as the Corporate Governance Code is not a source of law but merely a set of recommendations), in that the primary focus is the benefit of the shareholders, even though in the long term and in so doing, the directors should take into account also other stakeholders' interests.

What about legislation on directors' duties to stakeholders in other European jurisdictions? Let us take into consideration France and Germany. In France, *Le Plan d'Action pour la Croissance et la Transformation des Enterprises* (*Loi PACTE*) has been adopted by Law 2019-486 dated May 22, 2019, *relative à la croissance et la transformation des enterprises.* Among other measures, it provided for the amendment of Article 1833 of the Civil Code, which changed the definition of a company and its scope by stating that directors shall manage the company according to its interest:

> taking into consideration *social and environmental challenges* of its activity.

In other words, differently from the Italian Civil Code, the directors of a company (any company, listed or not, big or small) are required to consider, in addition to the shareholders, other stakeholders, such as the environment and society at large. The legal structure, however, is similar to the one adopted by the UK Companies Act (see Section 5.7) because in both cases, stakeholders, differently from shareholders, have not been specifically given, by legislation, legitimacy to start a legal suit against the directors. Therefore, the new provision will definitely imply for companies to adopt procedures and processes to evidence consideration of the mentioned challenges, even though the consequences in terms of directors' liability are not clear as yet.[37] The same *Loi Pacte* additionally amended Article 1835 of the Civil Code, authorizing (not requiring) companies to identify a purpose—a mission. These

[37] For a comment on the new provisions: Conac (2019), p. 497.

two provisions apply to all companies regardless of size and type (i.e., they apply to both private and public companies).

With reference to Germany, since the *Aktiengesellschaft* was enacted in 1965, members of the *Vorstand* have been required to pursue the company's interest, so-called *Unternehmensinteresse*: this is a broad definition, which does not correspond to the shareholders' interest and the maximization of profits solely, but it also includes consideration of other stakeholders, such as creditors, employees, and also associations of private citizens and institutions or any subject that enters into a contract with the company, like banks. The assumption is that all these interests are critical to pursuing the interest of the company itself, which is meant as distinct and superior in comparison with the sum of all the interests of the shareholders. In other words, it is possible to define a German company as a stakeholder company because the directors' duties shall not be primarily oriented to the shareholders but shall also consider different stakeholders. Also, the German Constitution, dated 1949, strengthens this idea by providing that the law of property is bound to the common good. Finally, the Corporate Governance Code (DCGK), dated 2022, for listed companies, states that the board of directors (*Vorstand*) is responsible for managing the company in its own best interest (*Unternehmensinteresse*) (Principle 1); in addition, Principle 2, Recommendation A1, states:

> In addition to long-term economic objectives, the corporate strategy shall also give appropriate consideration to ecological and social objectives.

The practical consequence is that directors have even broader discretion (compared to other jurisdictions) in that they need to reconcile different and sometimes divergent interests. However, the German Federal Supreme Court (BGH) has specified that, despite the discretion to pursue political, ethical, or social interests, directors shall not disregard the success of the enterprise, which means the preservation of the share capital and making profits.[38]

6.4.7 Public Companies: The Supervisory Boards in the Three Italian Models

Going back to Italian public companies, with reference to the regulation of supervisory boards, there are several differences among the three models.

Starting from *qualifications*, in the traditional model, all members of the board of statutory (or internal) auditors must meet the professionality requirements: Article 2397 of the Civil Code requires that there must be at least one certified accountant, and all other members must be professionals or academics (in law or economics). In listed companies, pursuant to Legislative Decree N. 58/1998, honorability adds to this requirement. Under the vertical two-tier model, the Civil Code (Article 2409-

[38] See Rondinelli (2020), pp. 267–281.

duodecies) requires at least one member of the supervisory board to be a certified accountant; for all others, there are no mandatory professional requirements but only voluntary professional requirements. The same rule applies to listed companies, where only the honorability requirement is added. With reference to the one-tier board model, Article 2409-*octiesdecies* of the Civil Code requires that at least one member of the internal committee should be a certified accountant; others shall comply with the honorability and professionality requirements, to be mandatorily provided in the articles of association. The same rule applies to listed companies.

As for *effectiveness*, for listed companies in all the models, Legislative Decree N. 58/1998 (Article 148-*bis*) provides for limits to the cumulative functions fixed under the Consob Regulation as members of all supervisory boards shall devote the necessary time to carry out their functions.

With reference to *independence*, Article 2399 of the Civil Code requires that members of the board of internal auditors in the traditional model must not be directors nor have family relationships with the directors (also of other companies belonging to the same group) nor have employment, consultancy, financial, or professional relationships with the company (or other companies of the same group) that may undermine their independence. The same provision is contained under Legislative Decree N. 58/1998 for listed companies (Article 148). If the company adopts the two-tier vertical model, the Civil Code requires that members of the supervisory board must not be directors nor have employment or consultancy relationships with the company (or companies of the group); that is, there is no reference to family ties with the directors or to commercial or financial relationships with the company (Article 2409-*duodecies*). The result is that it is lawful to have two or more family members serving in the management and the supervisory boards, and this circumstance is not deemed by the legislature as undermining an effective supervisory function over the directors. In addition, based on the same model, it is lawful to appoint a creditor (e.g., a bank) or a supplier to the supervisory board. Contradictorily, however, if a company is listed, the same independence requirements provided for the traditional model shall apply to the two-tier board model, and reference is also made to family ties as well as commercial and financial relationships. In the one-tier board model, under Article 2409-*octiesdecies* of the Civil Code, members of the internal control committee must not be executive directors nor have family ties with them nor have employment, commercial, financial, or professional relationships with the company (or other companies of the group). The same rule applies to listed companies.

With reference to the *composition* of listed companies, *in the three models*, at least one member must be appointed by the minority shareholders; this member will automatically be the chair of the supervisory board. The same mechanism and percentages provided for directors apply (see Section 6.4.6.1 above). Likewise, in the three models, if the company is listed, at least 2/5 of the board's seats shall be reserved for the least represented gender.

What are the *powers and functions* provided by legislation for supervisory boards? In this respect, there are also differences among the three models. In both listed and nonlisted companies, if the traditional model is adopted, the board of statutory (or internal) auditors shall be in charge of supervising compliance with law and the bylaws of the company, the correctness of management, and the adequacy of the internal control, administrative, and accounting system (Article 2403 of the Civil Code). They must draft an annual report on the financial statements, which is to be submitted before the annual meeting of shareholders (Article 2429 of the Civil Code). Internal auditors must attend the general meeting of shareholders and all meetings of the board of directors and of the executive committee. If they breach this duty with no justification, the sanction shall be decadence from the office. In small companies, the board of internal auditors is also in charge of auditing accounts and financial statements. In the two-tier board model, the supervisory board approves financial statements and is in charge of overseeing compliance with law and the bylaws of the company, the correctness of management, and the adequacy of the internal control, administrative, and accounting system (Articles 2409-*terdecies* of the Civil Code). In addition, if so provided under the bylaws, the supervisory board may also be in charge of adopting resolutions on the company's strategic, industrial, and financial plans, as proposed by the directors. Members of the supervisory board *may* be present in meetings of the board of directors (this is not a duty, so there is no sanction) and in general meetings of shareholders (but no sanction is provided otherwise). In companies adopting the one-tier board model, the internal committee is in charge of supervising the adequacy of the internal control and administrative and accounting system and also of verifying the correct representation of business activity (Article 2409-*octiesdecies* of the Civil Code). Members must attend the board of directors' meetings as well as meetings of the executive committee and general meetings of shareholders but, unlike with the board of statutory (internal) auditors, no sanction is provided in the case of absence.

Especially if companies are not listed, the rules on supervisory boards differ with reference to the *legal instruments* provided to exercise oversight functions. In the traditional model, each member of the board of internal auditors is granted *individual powers* to conduct inspections in the offices of the company and to exercise control as each of them may think fit (Article 2403-*bis* of the Civil Code). The board may collectively ask for information from the directors regarding the general business and/or specific affairs of the company. In addition, the internal auditors may hire people at their own expense to exercise such powers more effectively. If the company is listed, the individual powers of the internal auditors extend to that of asking for information from directors, in addition to inspection and control powers (Article 151 of Legislative Decree N. 58/1998). In the two-tier vertical model, the supervisory board has no inspection or control power; it may collectively ask for information from the directors on general business and/or specific affairs (Article 2409-*quaterdecies*). However, if the company is listed, individual powers to ask for information are granted to members of the supervisory board, while the board, collectively or through an appointed delegate, may exercise control and inspection powers (Article 151-*bis* of Legislative Decree N. 58/1998). Finally, in the one-tier board model, the internal control committee is not granted individual powers or the power of inspection or control. Each member, being a director, may ask executives to deliver to the board information concerning management and business; this rule applies to directors in all models (Article 2409-*octiesdecies* of the Civil Code). If the company is listed, individual powers to ask for information are granted to members of the internal control committee, while the committee, collectively or through an appointed delegate, is granted the power of control and the power to conduct inspections (Article 151-*ter* of Legislative Decree N. 58/1998).

Therefore, comparing the three models, one can notice that the model that provides for stronger effectiveness in the exercise of supervisory functions, especially if the company is not listed, is certainly the traditional model. This conclusion arises considering the rules on professionality and independence requirements, the duty to attend all board meetings (which ensures an adequate information flow), the functions, the powers, and the legal instruments. With reference to legal instruments, in particular, it is worth mentioning that allocating individual rather than collective powers allows more flexibility and speed in their exercise and therefore enhances more effective supervision over the company and its board of directors. While allocating powers to the board collectively (as it is the case with the one-tier and the two-tier vertical models) implies the need to convene the board and to reach a majority in order to adopt any decision; this mechanism slows down any action and might also hamper it. As a matter of fact, practice shows that the traditional model is highly preferred: almost 98% of listed companies adopt the traditional model, although some important banks have recently switched to the one-tier model (e.g., Intesa San Paolo, UniCredit). In general, almost 500 companies out of 60,000 have adopted the one-tier model: they are medium to big companies (and also banks).

6.4.7.1 Public Companies: Duty of Care and Liability for Supervisory Boards

While there are differences in terms of requirements, powers, and legal instruments among the three models, supervisory boards must all comply with the *duty of care* in performing their functions. However, with reference to the board of internal auditors in the traditional model, the Civil Code requires them to comply with both professionality and care (see Article 2407 of the Civil Code), a higher standard compared with that provided for the other two supervisory boards, which merely requires the duty of care. This contrast can be explained if we consider that there are different requirements in terms of qualifications under the three models: as mentioned above (see Section 6.4.7), only in the case of the board of internal (or statutory) auditors that all members must meet the professionality requirements. It is therefore coherent that the standard of conduct is higher.

With reference to liability, however, in all models, members of the supervisory board are jointly liable with the directors for the acts and omissions of the latter where the damage caused to the company or to third parties would not have occurred had they (the supervisory boards) properly exercised their powers (see Articles 2407, para. 2; 2409-*terdecies*, para. 3; and 2392, para. 2, of the Civil Code). In other words, in case directors are held liable, members of the supervisory boards are not automatically liable but only in case additional evidence of lack of supervision occurred that could have avoided the damage.

6.4.8 Institutional Investors in Listed Companies

As explained in Section 6.4.1, institutional investors have been acquiring growing power in the share capital of Italian-listed companies. Therefore, taking inspiration from the United Kingdom, and also from Italy, the Italian Association of Institutional Investors adopted, in 2016, the *Stewardship Code* to provide a set of high-level best practices designed to promote discussion and cooperation with investee companies.[39] It supports and guides investment management companies (i.e., companies that manage institution investors) concerning monitoring, engagement, and voting actions within investee companies in relation to, particularly, the strategy and performance of an investee company, its ordinary corporate governance matters, its approach to corporate sustainability, and risk management. Being a set of recommendations, they are based on the comply-or-explain principle. The Code states that there is a fiduciary obligation by institutional investors versus clients and beneficiaries, which includes a duty to adopt a long-term strategy in their investment.

According to Principle 1, institutional investors should have a documented policy available to the public on whether, and if so how, they exercise their ownership responsibilities. Principle 2 provides that institutional investors should monitor whether their investee companies are being proactive in order to identify problems in advance and to minimize potential losses. To this end, the appointment of an adequate number of independent members, including minority members, within the boards of investee companies—as explained under Section 6.4.6.1, Italian legislation provides for so-called minority directors as well as "minority members in supervisory boards"—can serve as a method of monitoring, in case that the Investment Management Company foresees intervention procedures, in accordance with what established in Principle 3. Under Principle 3, institutional investors should establish clear guidelines on when and how they will intervene with investee companies to protect and enhance value. Principle 4 states that institutional investors should consider cooperating with other investors, where appropriate, having due regard to applicable rules on acting in concert. According to Principle 5, institutional investors should exercise their voting rights in a considerable way in order to ensure that these rights are exercised solely in the interest of investors. Finally, Principle 6 states that institutional investors should report on their exercise of ownership rights and voting activities and have a policy on external governance disclosure.

References

Assogestioni (2013) Principi italiani di Stewardship per l'esercizio dei diritti amministrativi e di voto nelle società quotate, at https://www.assogestioni.it/articolo/principi-italiani-di-stewardship

Behrend J (1873) Zur Reform des Actiengesellschaftswesens. Duncker und Humblot, Leipzig

[39] Assogestioni (2013).

Conac PH (2019) Le Nouvel Article 1833 du Code Civil Francais et l'Integration de l'Interet Social et de la Responsabilité Social d'Enterprise: Constat ou Révolution? Rivista Orizzonti del Diritto Commerciale 3:497–516

Consob (2023) Report on corporate governance of Italian listed companies. Statistics and analyses

Davies P (2001) Board structure in the U.K. and Germany: convergence or continuing divergence? www.ssrn.com

Hanse JL, Lonfeldt C (2014) Corporate governance in Denmark. In: Lekvall P (ed) The Nordic corporate governance model. SNS Forlag, Stockholm

Hopt KJ (1998) The German two-tier board: experience, theories, reform. In: Hopt KJ et al (eds) Comparative corporate governance. The state of the art and emerging research. Oxford University Press, Oxford

Jungmann CM (2006) The effectiveness of corporate governance in one-tier and two-tier board systems – evidence from the UK and Germany. Eur Company Financ Law Rev 3(4):426–474

Marghieri A (1929) Delle Società e delle Associazioni Commerciali. In: Commento, vol IV. Utet, Torino

O' Donnell C (1952) Origins of the corporate executive. Bull Bus Hist Soc 26(2):55–72

OECD (2003) Survey of corporate governance developments in OECD countries. Retrieved from www.oecd.org

Relazione del Ministro di Grazia e Giustizia e dei Culti (Mancini) od Esposizione dei Motivi del Progetto del Codice di Commercio pel Regno d'Italia (1878) Stamperia Reale, Roma

Ripert G, Roblot R (2002) Traité de droit commercial, 18th edn. L.G.D.J, Paris

Rondinelli M (2020) Il sistema di governance nella società per azioni tedesca. In: Pederzini E (ed) Percorsi di diritto societario europeo. Giappichelli, Torino

Stevens H (1886) The Dawn of British Trade to the East Indies as recorded in the Court Minutes of the East India Company 1599–1603. Henry Steven & Son, London

The Charter granted by Queen Elizabeth, founding the company, 31st December, 1600 (1893) The Register of Letters &c. of the Governour and Company of Merchants of London trading into the East Indies 1600–1619. Birdwood G and Foster W, London

Timmermans C (2003) Harmonization in the future of company law in Europe. In: Hopt KJ, Wymeersch E (eds) Capital markets and company law. Oxford University Press, Oxford, p 623

Troplong RT (1845) Comentario del contratto di società in materia civile e commerciale, vol I. Domenico Capasso, Napoli, pp 446–447

Vidari E (1888) Corso di diritto commerciale. Hoepli, Milano

MIX
Papier aus verantwortungsvollen Quellen
Paper from responsible sources
FSC® C105338

If you have any concerns about our products,
you can contact us on
ProductSafety@springernature.com

In case Publisher is established outside the EU,
the EU authorized representative is:
Springer Nature Customer Service Center GmbH
Europaplatz 3, 69115 Heidelberg, Germany

Printed by Libri Plureos GmbH
in Hamburg, Germany